APPROXIMATE KNOWING

The End of our Dogmatic View of Religion

Gene Wesley Marshall

APPROXIMATE KNOWING
THE END OF OUR DOGMATIC VIEW OF RELIGION

iUniverse books may be ordered through booksellers or by contacting:

iUniverse
1663 Liberty Drive
Bloomington, IN 47403
www.iuniverse.com
844-349-9409

ISBN: 978-1-6632-6280-6 (sc)
ISBN: 978-1-6632-6281-3 (e)

Library of Congress Control Number: 2024909591

Print information available on the last page.

iUniverse rev. date: 05/20/2024

Everything we know
is approximate knowing.
To know that what we know is approximate
leaves us curious to know more
about everything we do know.

My aim in writing this book is:
to make room for religion
among the extremes of both
anti-religious secularism and
anti-secular religionism.
What shall we call this?
Will the "secular religious" do?

GWM

"All knowledge is local, all truth is partial.
No truth can make another truth untrue.
All knowledge is part of the whole knowledge.
Once you have seen the larger pattern,
you cannot go back to seeing
the part as the whole."

Ursula K. Le Guin

TABLE OF CONTENTS

PART TWO: KNOWING PROFOUND REALITY WITH RELIGIOUS METAPHORS APPROXIMATELY

PART THREE: THE NARRATIVES OF CHRISTIANITY

INTRODUCTION:
THE LAND OF MYSTERY

"Approximate Knowing" is short for "Living in the Land of Mystery." Here is my poem about this Land of Mystery that surrounds us, interpenetrates us, and provides us with all our content for knowing:

We live in a Land of Mystery.
We know nothing about it.
We don't know where we have come from.
We don't know where we are going.
We don't know where we are.
We are newborn babes.
We have never been here before.
We have never seen this before.
We will never see it again.
This moment is fresh,
Unexpected,
Surprising.
As this moment moves into the past,
It cannot be fully remembered.
All memory is a creation of our finite minds.
And our minds cannot fathom the Land of Mystery,
much less remember it.

We experience Mystery Now
And only Now.
Any previous Now is gone forever.
Any yet-to-be Now is not yet born.
We live Now,
only Now,
in the Land of Mystery.

We Live in the Land of Mystery

This Land of Mystery is an enduring presence that can be felt in every moment if we are sensitive enough. And this Land of Mystery is an active agency rushing towards us as an All Powerful Profound Reality that we meet in the unstoppable flow of time. No one can speed or slow the Earth in turning. No one can lessen or increase the sun's rate of crashing hydrogen atoms into helium ash in this nuclear fusion furnace of hydrogen bombs 93 million miles away. This Land of Mystery is all powerful, unstoppable movement, as well as unimaginable—unknown beyond the capacities of the human mind to know. Surprise to humans characterizes this Land of Mystery. We know what we know approximately through what has happened, what is happening, and what may happen next, but the whole direction and quality of time remains mysterious.

The enlightenment of the Buddha can be described as leaving the karma of the acculturated mind for an experience of the bliss of equanimity within this profoundly real, always existing Land of Mystery. The new birth in Christianity can be described as healing the strife among our many finite devotions by a reconciling loyalty with this Land of Mystery which is both a Void ending every thing and an Everythingness that holds us in an all inclusive connection.

The Exodus from the caste systems of Egyptian slavery into a journey through the wilderness of continual re-socializing can also be viewed as an exploration of the blessing of living in that Land of Mystery that envelops us all.

Knowing this Land of Mystery is a paradox that provides a foundation in profound consciousness for thinking about what is true and what is not true, but all our captured truth is but an approximation of this Land of Mystery and we do not know how approximate our approximate truths may be.

Our Temporal Knowing in the Land of Mystery

Alongside this Ultimate Mysteriousness, we need better vision of a depth anthropology adequate for living in 2024 and beyond. We require being rooted in a vision of the *evolution of life* on planet Earth. Each of us is a relationship with every aspect of that evolution. Each of us are a relationship with everything. We are each a unique set of relationships. And we are joined in joint relationship with all the humans in our nation in relationship with all the other such joint relationships—including say Bangladesh. Such relatedness is the context for both our psychologies and our sociologies. And concerning all these complex relationships we have only an approximate knowledge.

The narrative of evolution begins about 3.5 billion years ago. The evolution story of life on Earth is relatively brief compared to the scope of the *physical emergence* of the entire cosmos. The start of the process of physical emergence is currently dated at 13.8 billion years ago. Compared with this immense process of physical emergence as well as with the also immense story of life on Earth, the narrative of the human species is quite short. Only a few million years ago do we find in the archeological record the brain size and throat structures in an upright-walking primate species that would make possible the development of oral language.

Art may have evolved before language, and mathematics may have evolved somewhat later than language. These three symbol-using social processes, art, language, and mathematics, have made possible a human consciousness that can reflect upon our own consciousness and thereby become aware of being conscious. Please note that these are social processes which evolved in community. With this additional awareness and resulting freedom, the human species has become able to shape the structures of its own social commonality. This commonality includes cultural forms for our consciousness, structures of political order for our group decisions, and patterns for living our common economic lives more skillfully. In this industrial era our common economic power has been stretched to include the destiny of the Earth itself for its possible glory and for a likely further grief.

Prior to the evolution of humans, many species developed "cultures" of common communication, of common "political" fabrics, and of common "economic" lives. Nevertheless, our human form of consciousness has made possible both "taking in" more awareness about our natural and social environments and "taking on" more responsibility for the future of our social environments and our natural environments. It is this unique "more" in the form and agency for our human consciousness that constitutes a truly major turn in the evolution of life on planet Earth.

After long and careful thinking, Thomas Berry claimed that the following three major phases constitute our context for an adequate anthropology: (1) the *inanimate **emergence***, (2) the ***evolution** of life on Earth,* and (3) the ***history** of the human form of Earth-life.* Berry gave the name, "cosmogenesis" to these three inter-dependent processes of emergence. Berry preferred the more *process* word "cosmogenesis" to the more *static* word "cosmos." In fact, Berry asked us to view the nature of all temporal "realities" as a "process"—an ongoing-ness rather than a static-ness. It may still seem strange to think of every atom, every galaxy, every item in our house, and every aspect of our own bodies as a process rather than a static object. Words like "object" and "substance" are, within this process-shift in awareness, given this new meaning: "a relatively slow process." Words tend to "stop time," but real time does not stop. Our process words give expression to that quality of Reality.

This shift in the imagining of "temporal realities" includes the awareness that all our thoughts are approximate. Each thought is a process moving from a past form to a future form. Each thought can becomes a better thought. No thought has dropped down from some world of permanent thoughts. Some thoughts are long-lasting like Jung's archetypes, but even these thoughts are cultural temporalities awaiting betterment.

Nevertheless, becoming aware of the enduring Mysteriousness that is constantly encountering us can also reveal to us what are better approximations from what are worse approximations with regard to our thoughtful approximations of that Final Mystery that is calling to us in our personal and social lives. It is not that we create what is more real. We only create better or worse approximations of expressing the enduring Profound Reality that always was and always shall be an Unknown—a Mysteriousness that is unfathomable to the human mind. In spite of all our thoughtfulness, Reality is more than an idea. Reality continues to be a real *Thereness* that "judges" which approximations of Reality are better and which approximations are worse. Our very best overviews are not Reality with a capital "R," but only our best rational approximations of this capital "R" Reality. Human have had many names for this capital "R" Reality: The Great Goddess, Yahweh, Abba, Allah, Brahman, the Eternal Tao, etc.

Our awareness of this Final Reality is rather easy to come by; we simply admit the Reality of it. Humility in relation to our Real Life is just a matter of giving up the arrogance of our pretenses to a completeness of thought. Also, deep changes in our approximations of Profound Reality come about not only by rational methods only but also by intuition —stumbling into some "revelation." I will say more about this later. This process of changing thoughtfulness in not anti-reasonable but exists alongside our reasoning that never stops. Yet as we watch our reason reasoning, something more mysterious is also taking place—our deep consciousness—another enigma we can never master.

In this process-conceived world of thoughtfulness, our new sociological visions now arrive in our minds as narratives that interpret the events of the past in order to project options for the future and enable decisions to be made in the present. In this context of these narrative meanings, we find Thomas Berry naming future prospects like the Ecozoic future and the Technozoic future. Each of these two futures is one of two options for choice to be made in the present. Neither is a prediction, and neither is a fate. Both are viable and possible options to be chosen by humanity in the present. Our past events provide content for understanding these options.

Berry does a similar naming of past and future eras of life on Earth. He contrasts the 65-million-year-old Cenozoic Era with a now emerging era he calls the Ecozoic Era in which humans have become a very prominent natural-Earth power whose choices matter in a whole-Earth way. These general thoughts have come to approximate for me an emerging anthropology, yet such narratives are never complete.

Philosophizing in a New Key

Another key source for an adequate anthropology I have found in Susan K. Langer's book *Philosophy in a New Key*—in which she made a lot more clear to me the essence of art, language and mathematics. These three activities of human intelligence distinguish the intelligence of the human species from the chimpanzee and other primates. We share so many of our genes with the chimpanzee that the human species can meaningfully be called "the third chimpanzee" [the other two being a pygmy chimp (the smaller species) and the larger species (the one we know best.)] These three living species have a common ancestor about 10 million years ago. Since that common ancestor lived, all three of these now-living species have been evolving to their present form—not merely the upright-walking, big brained human but also our more tree-living sister species.

Furthermore, art, language, and mathematics form a unity we might call "symbol using intelligence." We cannot fully understand what language is without understanding what art is and what mathematics is. Understanding better this trio of symbol-using activities can assists us to understanding better the difference between human intelligence and the many other aspects of our consciousness that we share with the other animals. The intelligence that is unique to humans is built upon the foundation of the basic mammalian intelligence. We humans are mistaken when we project upon those other living species an intelligence that is using the human symbolizing of art, language and mathematics. We are realistic when we give honor to our unique human gifts and live them honesty and boldly, taking stock of their destructive as well as their constructive uses.

Mathematics

Of these three symbolic forms, mathematics is the most abstract. Sometimes mathematics is understood as an abstract version of language, but some of the best philosophers of mathematics see something more extensive in mathematics than a type of language. While linguistic logic is a kind of math, and many math statements can be said linguistically, the whole of math is something more. The more-than-language philosophers of math see in non-Euclidean geometries, set theory, and so on a contemplative study of the ordering capacities of the human mind. Others suppose that mathematics is only a study or the order we are discovering in the patterns we are finding in nature. But the relation between nature and math can be understood the other way around. The order we find in nature originates in the human mind. We find order in nature, but the order we find is a human approximation of the "ORDER" that is there. We are seeing that some of the patterns of order invented by humans with our wondrously ordering minds can aid us in approximating the patterns of nature. And such approximate knowledge of nature is exceedingly useful for our survival and our optimal living.

Later we will discuss the truth tests of our scientific disciplines. For now let us view the nature of mathematics to be a highly abstract contemplative inquiry concerning the possibilities of the human mind for our self-conscious means of order. Also, mathematics is an enormous field of study—perhaps as immense as the field of linguistics.

Art

Art is also an enormous field of study. Music, and dance, are non-linguistic arts that have to do with time (virtual time and virtual emotion). These motions in sound or body symbolize using a kind of abstract fiction about the quality of our real emotions and our real passage through time. ***Dance*** creates virtual communications in bodily movements that are beyond words. ***Music*** is a flow of sounds that creates a virtual flow of feeling through time that is beyond words. Music can communicate among us an emotion-communicating symbolization of soundings we may recall, and we may join in drumming or dancing its rhythms, or in singing or otherwise sounding its tunes. We know that music can speak to us of our real lives.

Painting, sculpture, and architecture are non-linguistic arts that have to do with space (virtual space). Like dance and music these three types of art cannot be reduced to language.

Poetry, song, story, and drama are linguistic arts that have to do with events or narratives of meaning (virtual events). All the arts express a grounding in specific "existing." Mathematics is a highly abstract form of "knowing" compared with art or language.

Language

Language is also an abstraction, less abstract than mathematics, more abstract than art. The abstractions of language are especially equipped for highly practical purposes like calling the children to supper. Poetry is language made into an art. The best of poetry helps us reach into life eventfulness and drag out its further meanings. I am sharing these few sentences about human symbol-usage to create an impression of what symbols are and what symbols do for us as a human species. The intelligence of a chimpanzee is great, but conducted with another form of mental entity than the "human symbol" that stands for some aspect of our real living. The chimpanzee has another means of communication—signaling specific circumstances using a different mental feature than symbols. I am calling that general animal intelligence feature a use of "multi-sensory reruns." Humans also use multi-sensory reruns in tandem with our symbol using. But to understand language we need to notice its difference from that more simple, but still powerful mental process in the intelligence of all the complex animals.

Knowing, Being, & Doing

"Knowing, being, and doing" (KBD) is language for a primary dynamic within all consciousness—human consciousness, chimpanzee consciousness, alligator consciousness, worm consciousness, amoeba consciousness. Is there a tree consciousness? If there is, it will be found to also to have knowing-being-doing aspects. Using the human form of consciousness, we humans speak of these KBD aspects of all consciousness in all the following ways and more:

awareness—identity—freedom
attention—presence—intention
taking-in—self-awareness—putting-forth
encounter—formation—response.

The vast complexity of ways that our living processes of consciousness can be spoken about may be boiled down to these three high abstractions: "knowing—being—doing"—a pattern of order "seen" within this boundless human enigma for which we use this term "human consciousness." The gift of consciousness comes complete with knowing, being, doing aspects. And "doing" as this word is used in this narrative includes response-ability or freedom. Doing is consciousness putting forth in reality changes,

Furthermore, aliveness and consciousness are corresponding concepts. Every entity that is conscious is also alive. And let us also explore the truth of this sentence: every entity that is alive is in some measure conscious. We tend to ascribe to the other species a lack of consciousness, when what we are facing is only a less intense form of consciousness than that of which we humans are capable. Also, we have many of these lesser layers of consciousness within our own beings. These earlier layers of consciousness are foundational for our symbol-using capacities. Using the term "measure" to describe consciousness is a stretch, for we do not know how to measure consciousness. We just know intuitively that human consciousness is somehow "more" than cat consciousness, and that cat consciousness is somehow "more" than worm consciousness. Furthermore, every word of language we use to describe consciousness is an approximation of that real consciousness of our consciousness that our mere words can never fully describe.

A Prelude of this Book

Nevertheless, in this book I will use plain human words (often using them metaphorically) to describe consciousness and even a profound consciousness of that Profound Reality of which profound conscious is conscious. What we must see first of all is how human consciousness is built upon mammalian consciousness and mammalian consciousness is built upon the forms of consciousness that preceded it in the evolution of living on planet Earth. Following is a brief description of the contents of this short book.

Section A of Part One

In this section I explore in more depth what I introduce in this introduction. I continue to sketch an emerging anthropology of consciousness using some ancient contemplative wisdom from India called "the seven chakras." I compare this Sub-Asian contemplation of human consciousness with seven stages of human evolution revealed in the contemporary evolutionary sciences. The evolution of the surprisingly intelligent octopus is another story from the narrative we must tell of the human story. The octopus lineage and the vertebrates separated from one another very long ago.

Section B of Part One

In this section I explore four different human approaches to approximate truths of the Ultimate Truth that we know we don't know fully with our finite minds. Nevertheless, we have a direct connection with this Unknown Reality touched by our deep or profound consciousness.

These four approaches to truth first came into my awareness in dialogue with the writings of the philosopher Ken Wilber who gave me an understanding of three distinct approaches to truth: (1) the *It-approach to truth* [the objective science approach], (2) the *I-approach to truth* [the interior contemplation approach] and (3) the *We-approach to truth*. I have broken down the we-approach to truth into two *sub-approaches to truth*. Here are my names for them: (3a) *the interpersonal approach to truth* and (3b) *the social commonality approach to truth*.

Further in section B of Part One, I explore how these four approaches to truth are unavoidable—they are all four participated in by every human being, however unaware most people may be in seeing that their knowing is taking place in these four separate ways or these four types of knowing.

I also spell out how these four approaches to truth cannot be rationally reduced into one another. Yet each one of the four remains an approach to that One Overall Profound Reality of Absolute Mystery. This means that the human mind is incapable of ever achieving a total rational grasp of the Full Truth. The best that we humans are able to do is to strap together these four separate pools of approximate truth into a practical overview that we have gathered so far in our particular life journey. This limitation in our thinking need not discourage us in being thoughtful persons; rather, these very limitations can provide us with some guidelines for thinking more clearly.

Section C of Part One

In Section C of Part One, I combine the evolutionary time quality of the seven layers of human intelligence with the intellectual separations or spacings of the four approaches to truth, thereby creating a narrative of historical development for each of these four approaches to truth. This organizing of an overall view into these four historic narratives can be helpful clarifications for the realistic living of these complex times with better approximations of the truth of this Mysterious Profound Reality.

Part Two: Knowing Profound Reality with Religious Metaphors Approximately

Part Two of this book is about religion—religion that has a vast number of different efforts for giving approximate expression to the inexpressible experience of that One overall Profound Reality—the Reality that is an "Encountering Eventfulness" of "Awe" that each of us is up against, confront, encounter, and might respond to in every moment of our lives. Profound Reality sustains us. Profound Reality is also that *Void* out of which each of us have come and into which each of us will return. This *Void* is also an enduring companion in which our aware life will swim in each living now. As we walk our walk from birth to death, Profound Reality walks with us. This deep abyss of a Void of nothingness is to both left and right, behind and before of our path through time. Oblivion is a part of aliveness.

Paradoxically, Profound Reality is also that *Fullness* that connects everything into the Whole of which we are a tiny part. This Whole includes our freedom to respond, our response-ability for our own lives, for the lives of all humans, for all life on this planet, and for all the Earth-processes that support life and bring all life to a close. Possibilities for living more fully is also a part of aliveness.

Void and *Fullness* comprise for us a *Total Demand* for awareness and response in the history of this species within the scope of all space and within the insistent flow of time.

Religion is not itself Profound Reality, but a mere human down-to-Earth practice that some people do—do together, do alone, do regularly. Religion is more than an identity, more than a subculture to which people belong. Our practice of a religion is somewhat similar to our practice of a piano or a violin or a clarinet. Yet religion is a different practice than playing a musical instrument or creating a painting. We practice a good religion for the sake of assisting us to be more immediately aware of Profound Reality and for assisting us in the acting out of our lives from our states of profound awareness and profound freedom that the aware presence of Profound Reality affords us. Obedience to realism is also a part of our aliveness possibilities.

In other words, there is nothing Eternal about a religion, yet an effective religion can assist us to be in touch with the Profound Reality that is the Eternal, lasting, all-encompassing, Final Reality.

Part Three: The Narratives of Christianity

Part Three is about Awe and the Awesome occasioned by Old and New Testament stories. It is also about the Awed Ones who confront the Awesome and are filled with Awe. Finally, it is about the ongoing theologizing in the 21st Century of Christian thoughtfulness based upon the event of the Christ Jesus revelation.

The stories of the Christian Bible are explored as religious practices that call forth the basic enlightenment occasioned by human-made proclamations called, paradoxically, "The Word of God" whose communications are beyond words. We call these communications with our species "revelation"—historically happening exposures of this Mysteriousness that remains mysterious. Christian theologizing is a religious practice that may be done weekly in an established congregation or in an intimate Circle of ex-laity and ex-clergy pioneering new form of Christian life-together. Similar theologizing is going on in Judaism and Islam.

Much more will be explored on these topics in Parts Two and Three. But first let us in Part One explore the foundations in human naturalness, beginning with our natural human intelligence.

PART ONE

The Evolution and Presence of the Natural Intelligence in the Human Species

Our human consciousness in not an invasion from above the natural realm, but a natural feature of our temporal lives. Even when our natural consciousness becomes aware of Profound Reality it is still a natural conscious becoming profoundly aware of the Profoundness that meets us in our every day lives. Part One provides some detail on what these sentences mean. I will explore these three topics:

A. Seven Layers of Natural Intelligence
B. Four Paths Toward Approximating the Mysterious Truth
C. Interfacing of the 7 Layers of Section A with the 4 Approaches of Section B

SEVEN LAYERS OF NATURAL INTELLIGENCE

U SING THE WORD "INTELLIGENCE" TO refer to a machine is an insult to natural intelligence. The natural intelligence of a worm is characterized by a level of awareness and initiative that is held by no device of so-called "artificial intelligence." AI can be remarkable useful, but it is not like the human intelligence that uses it.

The evolution of our complex natural intelligence beings began 3,500,000,000 years ago with the dawn of life on this planet. A second key date for human evolution is 65,000,000 years ago with the extinction of the larger dinosaurs opening up the flourishing of the resulting Cenozoic Era with flowering plants and birds and then mammalian forms of life flourishing approximately 40,000,000 years ago.

By 7,000,000 years ago some primate species began walking upright. By 2,500,000 years ago, we see the expansion in relative brain size within the homo set of species of upright-walking primates. And about 200,000 years ago modern humans began walking, running, talking, and organizing on this planet—replacing the other forms of upright-walking primates. All these dates are somewhat approximate—each of these shifts has build ups and follow afters that offer more fine-tuned dating. So, let us view the dates I cited as a kind of poetry about our origins—a scientifically-backed overview of the "time of our lives" as a species of life on planet Earth.

Detailed, contemplative, inward-looking reflections became significantly more present in India shortly after 800 BCE. As this style of careful inward research unfolded, we find the intriguing model of the seven chakras—a view of our human natural intelligence as swirls of awareness and active choice-making located symbolically from the base of our spine to the top of our head. I am going to relate this contemplative poetry to our story of evolution as constructed by contemporary biological and archeological science. It is interesting to me that these seven layers of consciousness are stacked along the human spine in that same 1 2 3 4 5 6 7 order as the unfoldment of life toward human life on planet Earth. And these seven swirls of potential human aliveness are natural features, not invasions from some supposed spirit world. The chakras of the human body and the evolution of life on earth are different stories about the same dynamics of being alive. I am going to describe all seven chakras briefly, relating the seven chakras with steps in the evolution of human life on planet Earth.

1. Survival

Chakra level 1 of our natural intelligence I am naming "Survival" to indicate an informed drive within all alive beings toward remaining alive. This intelligence for survival includes an awareness of the environment and some responsive capacities not found in a rock. The behavior of a tree must not be lumped in with the rocks. A tree, along with all multicellular plant life and fungal life, bends its branches and extends it roots in order to optimize its aliveness. We do not commonly call this consciousness, and it is certainly not the consciousness of consciousness experiences that are possible for human beings. But a tree is an animate being with some sort of sentience—with some sort of inward activity not present in a rock This basic impetus to choose options for life enhancement is also present in humans and in all animal life. Chakra 1 intelligence is as important for optimizing human life as it is for those majestic trees. And perhaps it helps for humans to know in order to enhance aliveness on this planet that we share with those trees about 25% of our genes. And without these friendly trees along with those single-celled algae pumping oxygen into the air, our form of life would not be possible.

2. Sensuality

To chakra level 2 of our natural intelligence I give the name "sensuality." We humans share this level of awareness and active impetus with all living beings that move around under their own power. This aliveness has to do with how to avoid pain, seek pleasure, and simply find our way about with whatever bodily sensibilities we have of our environment. Many forms of life have a smell sensibility much more highly developed than the smell capacities that have evolved in humans, yet forms of sensibility to the environment and to the internal processes of our biology are present in all animal species, including humans. Our sexual passion is an aspect of this swirl of natural intelligence. With regard to both chakras 1 and 2, I am describing a natural intelligence that is still without a consciousness of consciousness. For that reason we have often called chakra 2 consciousness "instinctual" rather than "self-conscious," but "instinctual" does not need to mean something mechanical or material rather than something creatively intelligent. The Charka poetry sees this intelligence located along the human spine in the genitals vicinity. Being aware of our sensuality is optimizing for a human life; it means some advantages to knowing ourselves better to

3

become more conscious of our sensual and sexual intelligence along with our becoming conscious of our later evolved layers of types of consciousness.

3. Purpose

To chakra level 3 of our natural intelligence I give the name "purpose." This is a gut-level mode of practical intelligence that we humans share with all the other complex animals. What we mean by "complex animals" may be a bit fuzzy: so let us at least suppose that the life of a worm is complex, and the life of a virus or an amoeba is not as complex as a multi-cellular worm, much less a chimpanzee or an octopus. Chakra 3 includes memory of the past and anticipation of the future, as well as the application of those wisdoms to the selection of our purposes of action. At this 3rd chakra level of natural intelligence, we are not yet referencing language, art, and mathematics. At this 3rd level of awareness we are not using the mental or thinking "tools" we call "symbols" found at the Chakra 5 level of our natural intelligence. Yet at the chakra 3 level of natural intelligence, we animals are doing purposive thinking using mental forms we might describe as "multi-sensory reruns"—the memories of sights, smells, tastes, sounds, and touches—that are rerun as images of remembered experiences that can be used in quite amazing ways by all the reptiles, birds, and mammals. These common abilities makes possible an ordering of memories into anticipations and purposes for practical responses that enhance our survival and optimize our living.

When we humans bat a base ball or play a game of tennis we are mostly using this chakra 3 level of intelligence. We are not using language in most of these actions. We may use language for thinking about these games ahead of time and afterward, but in the act of playing we are just an animal using this chakra 3 level of intelligence to move a bat or a racket. At this chakra 3 layer of our natural intelligence, we are communicating with one another through signs not words, not art forms, not numbers or geometric figures. We share this powerful chakra 3 development of natural intelligence with cats, dogs, horses, and whales as well as with lizards, turtles, snakes, octopi, sharks, and fishes.

4. Emotion

To chakra level 4 of our natural intelligence I am giving the name "emotional intelligence." This is our "heart chakra" as it is called— our capacity for bonding with other humans, animals, plants, and inanimate places, things and processes. We share this gift of awareness and freedom with all the mammals. We can bond with our cats, dogs, horses, and whales. Even cows have best friends. All mammals bond with their young. Even those big lonely male bears have a heart of feeling compared with a turtle, snake, frog, or shark. The shark has an incredible sense of smell and a very effective chakra level 3 intelligence, but no bonding capacity with humans. That animal can bites off our leg with no register of emotional sentiment whatsoever. Aquatic mammals, however, can bond with humans surprisingly well.

This emotional intelligence is far more valuable to us than we often notice. With our typical overemphasis on language, art, and mathematics, we often shield ourselves from noticing the full powers of our emotional intelligence. Or we count some of our emotions, such as anger, as inappropriate happenings, rather than as mere information from our bodies about the relation of our currently supposed self to our approximately understood environment. What we suppose about our self can be delusory, and what we suppose about the environment can be wrong, but the feelings that the body registers in emotional feelings are only information. However painful or unwelcome an emotion may be, it is just information that we can welcome, let rise, let endure a while, and let pass away. If we are stuck in some emotional mood or pain, we may need the assistance of a therapist to help us discover what "supposing" our mind may be inappropriately holding. All emotions are good information and need to be accepted and trusted. And all human persons—not just children, not just women, not just the old and dying—are in deep need of their emotional intelligence to optimize the navigation of our lives. My intent here is only in assisting us to identify the 4th or heart charka of natural intelligence. A full exposition of our emotional intelligence might require a whole shelf of books..

5. Symbolism

To the chakra 5 level of our natural intelligence, I give the name "symbol-using intelligence"—this intelligence is given its power through the uniquely human gifts of language, art, and mathematics. We often call this level of natural intelligence "thinking," but the real process of thinking includes a wider set of intelligences, especially chakras 3, 4, and 6. intelligences. Our thinking is also undergirded by chakras 1 and 2 as well as enhanced by chakras 6 and 7. All the complex animals have capabilities for "thinking." Humans clearly use chakra 3 capacities to do our practical, sense-related thinking. These earlier evolved modes of thoughtfulness undergird our more abstract symbol-using capacities that are present in the facilities of language, art, and mathematics. These insights about the interrelations of these 7 chakra qualities and abilities are crucial for our proper relations with our own bodies and with the natural world. Thinking is a very important augmentation for our survival, as well as an optimization of our aliveness.

In our reflections on chakra 7 we will be reflecting on what it is like to leave thinking behind and step off, poetically speaking, into the world of Wonder. Yes, living in the vast Land of Mystery will include doing some metaphorical thinking based upon our chakra 7 states of conscious intelligence, and this will reveal the fragileness of all our thinking. But however fragile and often flawed our thinking may be, when our chakra 5 natural intelligence is well supported by the other six swirls of natural intelligence, we do our best thinking, our best talking, our best writing, as well as our best art production and our best religious innovating,

Chakra 6 and chakra 7 are understood to be present only in humans—made possible by the symbol-using capacities found in chakra 5. The 6th and 7th forms of natural intelligence are faster swirls of awareness-&-freedom than chakra 5, but this does not mean that they are unnatural or supernatural. They are still natural—biologically assisted capacities given to every human baby.

7. Awakenment

6. 3rd-Eye Intuition

5. Symbolization

4. Emotion

3. Purpose

2. Sensation

1. Survival

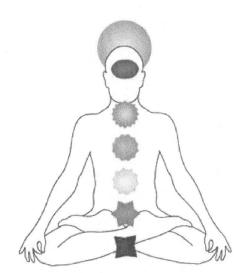

6. 3rd-Eye Intuition

Chakra level 6 of our natural intelligence is about "seeing" and "hearing" beyond our language using, art production, and mathematical ordering capacities. We sometimes call these 6th-level natural functions "intuition." Therapists sometimes speak of "listening with the third ear." The poetry of the Sub-Asian chakras have called this "seeing with the third eye" and have pictured this swirl of awareness and freedom as enabling an inter-human communication located in the center of the human forehead.

Our overemphasis in Western culture on the rationalities that characterize charka 5 has tended to minimize the importance of intuition—perhaps dismissing this form of natural intelligence as something magical—something given to only a few, mostly women. But intuition is just another down-to-Earth aspect of the gift of human consciousness. Everyone of us can enjoy intuitional "seeing" beyond our symbol-using thinking.

We get a glimpse of this level of awareness and freedom in the gaps between changing our minds from this to that. It is not just the Einstein-capable minds that allow consciousness to face the gaps between a previously taken-for-granted paradigm and a shift to another whole way of considering some key topic. We should not be afraid of those moments when we see visions that our culturally-conditioned eyes do not see. These gifts of pre-thought or post-thought insight are part of our natural intelligence. In the way I am using the word "intuition," I am speaking of something present only in the human being. Intuition is human symbol-using reaching out toward wonder. Or intuition is wonder calling to human symbol-using to reach out to wonder.

My favorite illustration of the power of intuition is found in the life of the physics-genius Einstein. He was a master of the gifts and the holes in Newtonian physics reaching out toward his surprisingly wonder-filled person for the intellectual space to create a new physics. Einstein used the word "intuition" to describe his work of seeing a whole new universe that turned out to be verified by observations.

There may be other ways that the word "intuition" is being used, but the intuition I am am pointing to with the chakra 6 description of 3rd-eye awareness is a gift of the human to reach beyond human rationality. A chakra 5 gift of intelligence is needed in order to have this 3rd-eye of our natural consciousness—something in our basic make up that our more intense life forms uses our chakra 5 capacities. We might say that intuition is a consciousness of consciousness itself and its creative powers. And this awareness of being conscious of consciousness and is thereby aware of that of which consciousness is aware.

When philosophers claim that the rational is the real, they are denying the irrational enigma of our own consciousness and the irrational Mysteriousness of that Profound reality concerning which our profound consciousness can be aware and free beyond the limitations of the human mind. A rational-is-the-real philosopher is delusional to suppose that the patterns of Reality that currently form his or her mental confidence are Reality—or that human mental powers will ever be capable of encompassing the Profound Reality that we do actually confront now with our enigmatic consciousness if we are willing to consult our sensitivities for doing so.

Also important, these chakra 6 and 7 insights holds no contempt for the human mind; it only puts the human mind is its proper place—namely, that our rational universes of thought are, at best, approximations of Profound Reality. This insight also helps us separate the meaning of the word "consciousness" from the more limited meaning of the word "mind." We will continue in this book saying how important that is.

We will also explore how consciousness in all its forms is not an invasion of a supernatural realm. All seven of these chakras are just our natural lives. Consciousness is a finite process as well as mind. Yes, consciousness cannot be directly seen scientifically, and nor can mind, as understood as the subjectively viewed functioning of the human brain and nervous system. Scientifically, we only see outwardly the brain and nervous system as well as the behaviors of the animal. Also, we cannot "see" with science alone how the mind sometimes functions without conscious intentions and sometimes does obey conscious intentions. These are contemplative insights. The mind regulates biological functions and automatic behaviors that never need conscious attention. Consciousness shows its independence from mind when it uses the functionality of the mind for intended purposes. It is consciousness that both *knows* reality and that *does* the basic reality changing. When we speak of "doing" we commonly mean consciousness is using the mind to preform a consciously intended action. Looking from the place of this awareness, the mind can seen as somewhat like a computing tool—an amazing biological tool much more capable in some ways than the most advanced computers. Finally, neither mind nor consciousness can comprehend the boundlessness of *Reality*.

Chakra 6 is a natural intelligence that knows both the limits of consciousness and the limits of mind as well as the boundlessness of the Profound Reality being encountered by consciousness. Mind is a type of tool that enabled consciousness to reflect upon all these matters and thereby become more conscious through being aware of consciousness itself. Herein is a sense of how chakra 5 natural intelligence is a foundational step toward chakra 6 natural intelligence.

Third-eye intuition (chakra 6) is not in any way something supernatural. The chakra 6 capacities for intuition is a completely natural level of being aware and free. This 6th level of natural intelligence is like a "larger space" than the chakra-5 symbolizing reflections. Let us call this seemingly strange *spaciousness* "being aware of consciousness itself" as something more than mind. This is not a rejection of mind: it is a viewing of mind from a larger scope of awareness. Accessing this expanded consciousness can give us a quality of looseness from what we now take to be "real" in a larger way than the "real" that is limited to rational knowing. Also intuition is a wider and deeper view of Reality than rational order. And the power of intuitive imagining has a great impact on the rational, especially upon our seeing beyond our current ways of ordering to new and more powerful ways of ordering—and thereby upon larger scopes for our ethics and our everyday behaviors. Within this space of intuition, our thinking skills can then come back into play in wider ways. After our trip into the intuitive space we can build new frames for our practical living. These insights are very important for our social revolutionary thinking and for our openness to experiencing chakra 7 intensities of natural human consciousness.

7. Wonder

The chakra 7 level of our natural intelligence is about our capacity for "Wonder" or "Awe." These two words can be used in trivial ways, but at best they point to profound states of our consciousness—an ability to be open to the presence of "*That Awesome Wholeness*" that is beyond our understanding—"*That Land of Mystery*" in which we subsist—"*That Surprising Future*" that we cannot prevent from occurring but that demands our responses—*that Eternal Now* that breathes aliveness to our being. However mind-blowing it is to give language to our 7th-chakra-level experiences, we are speaking of a layer of our natural intelligence that no human being is without. Nevertheless, we may be suppressing the wonder part of our conscious lives. Or perhaps we are only recently finding the wonder part of our lives, having not uncovered it before.

Whatever be the state of our wonder experiences, we have no need to suppose that experiences of wonder or awe are supernatural invasions of our natural lives from some super realm. Symbols like "Holy Spirit" need not mean something spooky or in any sense an invasion of our natural consciousness. "Holy Spirit" can simply mean "awed natural consciousness"— an enhancement of our ordinary human consciousness—like being "set on fire" with the wonder that can occur in our natural consciousness in the presence of the Wonderful. We can be experiencing awe in the presence of the Awesome without making the Awesome meaning another universe. I am going to explore seeing the Awesome as the Lastingness happening in the midst of the temporal, and I will spell that out far more completely as I move on. This Lastingness is a type of "otherness" to our temporal experiences that do not last. But this otherness is part of the one universe of Reality. We do not need the metaphor of two universes of Reality. We only have two realms of thoughtfulness the wonder experiencer and the Wonderful that is occasioning the wonder.

Also, "wonder" can mean a very wide variety of states— a mild sounding state of fascination appropriate for words like "rest" or "peace "or "joy." And "wonder" can also be an intense dread, or deep challenge, or an overwhelming calling to risky action. The Wonderful is not always beautiful, or nice, or non-violent. When wonder does manifest as a state of simple beauties, this may mean something very profound— that we are no longer fighting with Reality, or fleeing from Reality, but making friends with a Reality viewed as benevolent. "Wonder" means touching with our natural consciousness the *Fullness of Reality*, rather than adoring some self-created fiction, or imagining confronting a sugar daddy that replaces the more horrifying Yahweh of Hebraic scripture. Yahweh is a personalized metaphor for the Wonderful and we Christians need our Old Testament severities to have a complete view of the Wonderful Awesomeness that does simply happen in our chakra 7 level of natural experiences.

Further, let us note that "estrangement from Reality" is not created by Reality, but by you and me and the many group efforts of our shared humanity in lusting for a life different from Reality. Reality may seem angry to us, but Reality is only being Reality. It is human freedom that is the source of our estrangements from Reality. The Reality we face also includes the results of our rebellion from Reality. If we kill someone, they remain dead. If we lead society in a wrong direction, that results in something others may be called to correct later. And many such results eventually lead to a very real despair we cannot throw off in our own despairing state. But this despair is a doorway—an indicator of the delusion that needs to be given up in order to return to the blessing of realism, a gift of that Real Reality that is always welcoming the wayward ones home to realistic living.

"Wonder" or "awe" are names for this 7th and "fastest swirl" of our seven-layered natural intelligence. Wonder is a gift given to us in the everyday history of our personal, natural, and social events. The *Wholly Otherness* of Profound Reality, when present to us is experienced as awe or wonder. We humans are not always open to experiencing this *Wholly Other* as our *Real Holiness.* But wonder, however grim or however pleasing, is *something human*, essentially so. When these awe-filled moments do occur, we may be reluctant to see them as beneficial for us, strength for us, blessing for us, so we push awe away, ignore it, and/or deny its presence. Our best case life is the wonder-filled life.

Finally, the language that we humans have to throw around to describe chakra 7 is of necessity metaphorical rather than literal. Nor are chakra 7 experiences simply ideas or states of living we have made up or caused to be. Chakra 7 awarenesses are parts of the Reality that is coming at us. In my moments of awe, I am sharing aspects of what is actually being given to me. Experiencing *Wonder* includes a surrender of what is blocking Wonder, rather than some accomplishment of my own strength. And if *Wonder* is absent from our life, we might ask ourself "What is blocking the *Wonder*." In almost every case the blocking feature is some form of self promotion of some sort of imagined self that is nothing more than an imagination —a self image that is being substituted for that *Wonder*-experiencing being that we actually are beneath all our layers of escape. Wonder is an openness, a surrender to Reality, a finding of our own actual deepest truth.

Our typical imaginary self is composed of various rational beliefs and moral patterns that define our self image. This self image is a living reality that is defending and promoting this substitute "me." To give up this self image (which is a living lie) can therefore be a death-like experience. But such death is also a release from prison—the prison of the deluded self. Let us take note of these excerpts from the D. H. Lawrence poem "New Heaven and New Earth"

> At last came death, sufficiency of death,
> and that at last relieved me, I died.
> I buried my beloved; it was good, I buried myself and
> was gone.
>
> . . . . .
>
> and I am dead, and trodden to nought in the smoke-
> sodden tomb:
> dead and trodden to nought in the sour black earth of
> the tomb;
> Dead and trodden to nought, trodden to nought.

God, but it is good to have died and been trodden out,
Trodden to nought in the sour dead earth.
quite to nought,
absolutely to nothing
nothing
nothing
nothing.

For when it is quite, quite nothing, then it is everything.
When I am trodden quite out, quite, quite out,
every vestige gone, then I am here
risen, and setting my foot on another world
risen, accomplishing a resurrection
risen, not born again, but risen, body the same as before,
new beyond knowledge of newness, alive beyond life,
proud beyond inkling or furthest conception of pride
living where life was never yet dreamed of or hinted at,
here in the other world, still terrestrial,
myself, the same as before, yet unaccountably new.[1]

Awe is the death of who you have been thinking that you are. Our delusions are invisible to us who still have them, for to see our practices of self promotion is seeing that they are a sort of lie. And seeing that a lie as a lie is an experience of truth. The lucid Buddhist may be naming this experience as "enlightenment." "Enlightenment" is a sort of poetry, but it is not a fantasy, it is descriptive of an experience of realism. The Christian may be naming these same experiences "new birth," "spirit healing," "salvation," or with some other sort of poetry.

---

[1] Lawrence, D. H., *Selected Poems*, New York: The Viking Press, 1959: page 77,78 copyright 1916

Such metaphorical language may point to experiences that overlap with "enlightenment." Buddhist and Christian poetries, though quite different in terms of their metaphorical speech, can, nevertheless, provide a type of bifocal "seeing" of the same basic experiences. But, I am getting ahead of a more orderly unfolding of my thoughtfulness about religion. I will discuss religion more thoroughly in Part Two of this small book.

In this quick description of the 7th chakra consciousness, I am attempting to describe how 5th charka thoughtfulness is useful in describing 7th chakra states of awareness and freedom. Our thoughtfulness today about the 7th chakra consciousness can dispense with the metaphor of a supernatural world of Spirit Beings invading the natural universe. Instead, we can view this 7th level of consciousness as touching with our consciousness into the "Oneness of Profound Reality"—the Reality we experience in our everyday lives as the depth truth about the manyness of events that comprise our ongoing experience of this single cosmogenesis of processes. We do not glorify some other realm, and we do not demean this one realm of Reality. We find the sacred, the Awesome, the Holy, here and now in the midst of all our ups and downs of temporal events.

These 7th chakra descriptions are about a real layer of our natural intelligence that can be experienced by our natural consciousness. This 7th intensity of natural intelligence can be experienced within the *Oneness* of actual living that is possible for every human being in every culture. Our finite minds can use metaphors taken from the manyness of nature and history to reach beyond those everyday words—coughing out insight using such time-bound metaphors without meaning these expressions literally. In other words, the mode of expression required for sharing our 7th chakra experiences must be done with a form of poetry—a fragile form of story-telling or word-stretching that allows us to tell about "*That*" which eye cannot see, nor ear hear, nor any other physiological sensibility encompass. Here is another bit of poetry that hints toward this 7th layer of human consciousness:

> I am an alert deer.
> Dread gets my attention
> and I can move quickly
> in many directions.
> I am a surprise
> and hard to predict.
>
> A fear of real enemies
> is the alertness of a deer,
> While my alertness is
> dread of a mysteriousness
> no deer can know.
>
> And I am unpredictable
> in a manner
> no deer can match.
>
> Dread of the Unfathomable
> is my essence.
>
> Surprise
> is my being.

A Conclusion about the 7 Chakra Levels of Natural Intelligence.

The above descriptions of the ordinary nature of human consciousness and of natural human intelligence as outlined in this seven-level chakra poetry is held, I believe, in the following Lakota prayer that I found on a tote bag. I have added chakra references to this prayer to show how we can see in this simple prayer the omnipresence of these seven chakra levels of our natural human intelligence.

> "Teach me how to trust my heart (chakra 4), my mind (chakra 5), my intuition (chakra 6), my inner knowing (chakra 3), the senses of my body, (chakras 1 & 2), the blessings of my spirit (chakra 7). Teach me to trust these things so that I may enter my sacred space and love beyond my fear, and thus walk in balance with the passing of each glorious sun (chakras 7 & 1)."

I find this prayer to be about these seven chakras. This is a bit surprising, but with eyes trained to see this chakra framing we can see the chakra insights in other ancient and contemporary poetry found throughout the planet. Numerous are the witnesses to this ordinary and natural scope of our natural intelligence and of the natural evolution of such awareness and freedom on planet Earth.

Finally, here is a conclusion we might draw from these reflections on the chakras of consciousness. Like gravity or electromagnetism, consciousness might be viewed as a field in the fabric of the cosmos. What this would mean is that on any planet in the cosmos on which conditions for biological organization arise, consciousness, like the space/time field of gravity, is a field of reality that might be accessed. Gravity is invisible in its way, but we can objectively measure its effects. And with Einstein's help we have come to see that gravity is not a suction from a distance but a curvature in the shape of space-time. And we have the measurements to show this advance in understanding to be true.

Measurements we do not have for consciousness. But perhaps we do have some awarenesses that the human qualities of consciousness in chakras 5, 6, and 7 are somehow "more" than the levels of consciousness we share with the other animals. We experience our consciousness of this "more" through our contemplative inquiry before we can see it also in our objective sciences. To the extinct that we view consciousness, we do so as an inward consciousness of the phenomena of consciousness. Without the agency of this inwardness or subjectivity, the outward events that manifest consciousness are invisible as consciousness. It is the inward intelligence of the cat that can notice the difference between a beetle and a rock.

Though our foundations in animal consciousness are huge, human inwardness builds on this inward intelligence of the other mammals a uniquely human form of consciousness and of that profound consciousness of Profound Reality. However powerful and "more" human consciousness may be, it is still a veneer on layers of consciousness (awareness and freedom) that are billions of years in the making before our species began its unique journey.

So, let us imagine that in the first million years of our emergence from our primate foundations, our biggest anxiety was sinking back into our immense animal womb. Many early hunter-gatherer groups may have done just that. Perhaps it was our fragile but remarkable culture building talent that established our foothold in being a stable form of being the human type of consciousness. That gift was found to be effective for out-performing the other upright-walking primates. Even if it was not always our intention to do so, our rise in consciousness killed them off with our choices to become and to live out the human form of consciousness.

We now face accessing our own profound consciousness and living from it in order to inspire any hope of survival for our species. And let us keep in mind that we make this intensification journey as a community of beings not merely as lone individuals. We also become strong individuals in community with millions of others. The image of "lone wolf" is neither wolf nor human.

FOUR PATHS TOWARD APPROXIMATING THE MYSTERIOUS TRUTH

E VERY HUMAN BEING PARTICIPATES, HOWEVER minimally or unknowingly, in four ways of *knowing approximately* the many contents of this overall *Land of Mystery*. These four ways of knowing never arrive at the full Truth, but they are means of approximating that full Truth and these approximations can be good enough to sustain and optimize our existence.

However clear we may be about how all our knowledge is approximate, we may also be blessed to notice the *glory* that our knowledge can be *an approximation of the Full Truth—of the Land of Mystery*. So let us not despair, as if we have no truth. We can even have better approximations than we used to have—seeing something better than we used to see it. Nevertheless, any desire of a finite human being to conceptualize and thereby own or somehow possess The Truth in a final sense is a form of arrogance that is doomed to be shot down by the way life is. Unreal living is also present in our camping out in some preferred holdings and perhaps choosing never to be curious about anything more ever again.

It is an important part of our commitment to realism that we maintain this important discovery that we are always, and will always be, vastly ignorant. Nevertheless, we are a very complex animal potentially aware of that this Mysteriousness of Profound Reality is open to increasingly better approximations of our knowledge of that Finality of Truth.

We humans are all scientists who know much about the objective world, contemplative inquirers who know much about the inner life, interpersonal beings who have learned to live with other persons, and socially alerted citizens who are capable of responsible acts of social maintenance or social changes that entails defining and fighting for causes of justice. All of us, not just some of us, participate in all four of these realms of approximate knowing. Yet no amount of this knowing changes the fact that we are also infinitely ignorant of any final knowledge of Reality.

We do not even know how approximate our four types of approximate knowledge may be. This ignorance remains true even among the most prominent scholars, contemplative inquirers, therapists, and social leaders among us. Still we may respect these leaders in thoughtfulness and their well-earned renown, in spite of the fact that they, just like all of us, are approximate knowers before the Full Truth of Reality. Indeed, we only have our awareness that our previous approximations are more approximate through gifts to us of those improved approximations.

The Full Truth is still beyond us and will always be beyond us. To say that we do not know whether we humans will ever know the Full Truth is a last ditch stand for the knowability of the Full Truth by the human mind. Indeed, let us assume that zero is the probability that there is out there sometime & somewhere in our human future that a full knowing of The Full Truth of Reality will be present. As finite humans, *we live in a Land of Mystery,* a mystery that does not go away. Students of modern physics have learned that instead of lessening the mystery of nature with our better physics, the mystery of nature has grown greater.

It may seem preposterous that we can say anything definite about *the essential human being* that transcends our vast differences in cultural development and also in our huge biological variety. Nevertheless, we can know a great deal of approximate wisdom that does apply to all humans. Though all our knowledge is approximate, we can confidently present the approximate truth that there are four types of knowledge as a viable place to begin to continue some clarifications on being approximately knowledgable persons about what it means to know Reality approximately.

1. The Scientific Approach to Truth

The scientific approach to truth is basic to every human being as one of our elemental paths to truth. An elemental form of science existed prior to Aristotle, prior to Pythagorus, and so on back. And Greece is not the only place for the origin of science. Perhaps the objective type of truth even had precursors in mammalian life or in still earlier forms of animal life. The human form of the scientific approach to truth has also had a long antiquity in the human form of science, and today we have a highly developed form off scientific truth that has become an unavoidable fixture in our modern lives for each and every one of us, even though some of us resist it. But resisting science is not necessary. What is appropriate practice is seeing that the scientific battery of truth is only part of the total picture of approximate knowing.

We are all scientists now. In recent centuries we humans have shared with Einstein, Darwin, and others. many sophisticated scientific findings that have astonished us, as well as baffled us. Nevertheless, the scientific approach to truth, vast and powerful as it has become, remains a limited approach to truth. We see this in sciences' own constantly changing qualities. We have also learned from recent developments in science itself that its objective methods make it a limited source of knowledge. The pure scientist does not study subjectivity. Science can study human behaviors and human reports that assume the presence of subjectivity, but the pure scientist is silent about his or her own subjectivity as well as not making a direct approach to subjectivity itself. To find a direct exploration of human consciousness, we have to look to those of us doing *contemplative inquiry*.

The scientific approach to truth is incapable of extending its means of truth verifying to three other quite different approaches to truth—contemplative inquiry, interpersonal savvy, and the commonality skills for the workability and justice of our societies. All four of these approaches to truth characterize the natural intelligence of the human species. I thank the philosopher Ken Wilber for alerting me to these four approaches to truth.[2]

I got my Batchelor's degree in mathematics and physics, and I have continued my interest in the study of the sciences and in the philosophy of science. Science is a method,, an ongoing search, not a set of truths found somewhere. So what is it that allows us to see that some bits of scientific truth as better than other bits of scientific truth? Here is a quotation about looking for a new physical law from a book by the Nobel Prize-winning physicist, Richard Feynman:

> *In general, we look for a new law by the following process. First we guess it. Then we compute the consequences of the guess to see what would be implied if the law we guessed is right. Then we compare the result of the computation to nature, with experiment or experience, compare it directly with observation to see if it works. If it disagrees with experiment, it is wrong. In that simple statement is the key*

---

[2] Wilber, Ken, *A Brief History of Everything*, Shambhala, page 107

*to science. It does not make any difference how beautiful
your guess is. It does not make any difference how smart
you are, who made the guess, or what his name is—if it
disagrees with experiment it is wrong. That is all there is
to it.* [3]

Feynman goes on to remark that we may need to recheck an experiment to see if it was done correctly. And he explains how this task of theory guessing is a sophisticated process, involving a knowledge of the known facts in the field of inquiry and some familiarity with the other theories already found right or wrong. But the plain truth of scientific research is spelled out in Feynman's colorful words. Scientific truth is just a guess waiting to be shown wrong. And the test of right or wrong to such guesses is found in the observations of physical nature itself by a peer group of human observers.

2. The Contemplative Approach to Truth

The contemplative approach to truth has to do with the inward look of our human consciousness, rather than the outward look of our human consciousness. We can intuit that looking outward scientifically and looking inward contemplatively are two means of looking at the same Land of Mystery. Yet for our knowledge of this One Final Reality, we do actually look both ways, and we must look both ways with our rational inquiries. Indeed, it is this inward being that is doing the outward looking. And it is the outward living human individual who is doing the inward looking.

Nevertheless, these two directions of looking are distinctly different

---

[3] Feynman, Richard, *The Character of Physical Law*, Cambridge MS: MIT Press, 1967. p 156

modes of inquiring about Reality, and these two inquiries result in two separate "filing cabinets" of our interior mental content. While our contemplative quest for truth is using the workings of the same outward brain and nervous system, the interior results of mental content are different from the results of outward looking.

The mysterious reality of consciousness is indeed looking both ways. By noticing this duality of looking, we are becoming more conscious of being conscious and with how consciousness is a deeper experience of our lives than the process of thinking. Thinking is as I will show, four different filling cabinets of knowing, but our consciousness of Reality is one consciousness relating to One Reality. Thinking is an activity of consciousness using the mind. Scientific research is consciousness looking outward. And contemplative inquiry is consciousness looking inward upon the patterns of consciousness itself.

We may not have noticed how different our memory recordings are between these two directions of looking. Here is an important example: understanding our experience of "time." In the inward contemplative approach to truth the time is always *now*, with the past being the *now* of memory and the future being the *now* of anticipation. In contemplative inquiry, *time* is a flow of events through this ever present *now*. But in the scientific approach to truth, *time* is a measurable length, along with three measurable dimensions of space. The *now* in the scientific approach to truth is an infinitesimal dot dividing the line of *time* into past and future. Both ideas of time are rational assumptions that fit their respective quest for truth, but not the other quest. Both are true within their own home quest. The data of each direction of looking is storied with this different concept of time attending each bit of data of each type of data.

This duality in our thinking is not a duality in Reality. The One Reality is simply being approached in two different ways, Each of us can notice this, and this noticing shows us that "the rational is not the real" and "the real is not rational." Rational is a human invention of approximation of the Real with a capital "R." And it takes these two patterns of rational thought to better approximate the Real. In fact, approximating the real takes four patterns of rational thought. I turn next to the last two. Ken Wilber calls both of the following two approaches to truth a "we" approach to truth. He contrasts them with the "it" approach to truth (scientific research) and the "I" approach to truth (contemplative inquiry).

3. The Interpersonal Approach to Truth

Vast as are the scientific and contemplative approaches to approximate truth, we find that we humans operate with two other approaches to truth, also, both vast for each of us. The first of these "we" approaches is the type of knowing that derives from our intimate relations with other persons. We might call this approach to truth "the interpersonal approach to truth." When two or more human persons share person-to-person living with each other, something more is happening than in the objective observations of the sciences or in the subjective inquires of the contemplative methods. When"I" meets another "I" (a "Thou" to me), we are experiencing a mode of living that is neither objective research nor subjective inquiry. Interpersonal truth is both objective and subjective, and it is neither.

An interpersonal relation begins as an encounter by my "I" with the expressions of another human "I" experienced by me as a "Thou." Martin Buber helps us see clearly that the encounter of Thou is a different type of encounter than an encounter with "it." When I make some sort of inwardly initiated response to a "Thou," that response becomes a "Thou" encounter to this other "I." Then this other person responds out of that person's subjectivity with an encounter with my "I." These thousands of interpersonal "case studies" produced by our interpersonal relations form another internal filing cabinet of mental products, basically different from the facts of science and the phenomena of inwardness.

This I-Thou-I Thou-I-Thou dialogue is a mode of thoughtful learning that is distinguishable from our scientific research and our contemplative inquiry. Scientific research has a peer group who test it, but these many eyes observe objects, rather than dialogues with persons. Similarly, our contemplative inquiry is shared with others, but each of the conscious beings who is involved in the inward inquiry is focused for knowledge validations upon their own contemplative inquires of their own inward verities.

The interpersonal approach to truth is a mode of learning that is taking place through time with a communal movement of encounter-and-response, encounter-and-response, encounter-and-response, until enough encountering and responding have gone on to make some sort of contribution to our interpersonal "mental filling cabinet." We tell most of this truth with stories or case studies. And these stories begin in infancy. Each of us began this type of learning before we could walk or talk, Furthermore, most humans have learned most of what they know in this interpersonal manner.

The infant is storing up I-Mama, I-Papa, etc. interpersonal beginnings of her interpersonal chest of memories. This interpersonal quality of truth and memory storage is vast and continues throughout our whole lives. This interpersonal savvy is an ever-present recall process that is never absent. It is ongoing throughout our lives. I am 92 and still learning about this dimension of my whole life.

4. The Commonality Approach to Truth

This fourth approach to truth applies to the understanding of our social environment. Let us notice our dependence upon sharing in a continuing learning from and creation of that environment, our repair of it, and our discontinuation of specific social processes of our inherited cultural, political, and economic processes. Cultural processes hold our consciousness in being, Political processes enable our group decisions, Economic processes enable us to best use one another and our Earth resources to make those Earth resources useful for humans. We then find ways of distributing those produced gifts and services to everyone (wisely or poorly). Nothing in our common social life is set forever, and we are communally responsible for our common life. "We" are responsible for what we have and for what we will continue to have as a social reality..

This fourth approach to truth is thoroughly mingled with the other three approaches to truth. This social dependence on the other three modes of truth is true to such an extent that it can seem like there is no independent fourth approach to truth; however, that is not so. Taking care of our social responsibility requires a distinct fourth mode of reflection and action that I am naming "the commonality approach to truth." Human society is part of our environment, just as nature is part of our environment, but the facts of our social environment are quite different from the facts of our natural environment.

Social processes are not natural process, even though we might say that it is natural for we human beings to create social processes. We might go father to say that it is natural for humans to create these three forms of social processes: economic processes, political processes, and cultural processes. It is, however, human choices rather than natural givens that creates the specific social processes that become our social environment.

For example, both a US democracy and a Russian fascism are human made. Let us not be confused by viewing either one as being simply "natural." This means that the facts of social history, because they are human made, create a social environment that has a very different character than the facts of the natural environment.. Nature is an environment that is not human made. Human agency is not present in the vast power of the Earth turn or the sun shine, but human agency is present in the economic system of a human society. For example, having billionaires and wretched poverty is not natural: it is humanly chosen. These simple truths make social facts a different sort of facts than the facts of physics, biology and other natural sciences.

Nevertheless, these human-made social factors of our human history of social processes have and must use the wisdoms we have found through our quests for scientific truth, contemplative truth, and interpersonal truth. Social history also requires that a fourth approach to truth be added to these other three approaches to truth. This fourth type of truth must be tested with a fourth type of test. My name for this test is "social workability."

Take for example the social truth involved in handing the climate crisis. It is obvious that the truths of the natural sciences have unearthed for our awareness of the climate crisis. These truths of the climate scientists are important knowledge for our understanding of this crisis., but the social factors of this challenge are something more than the scientific facts about the climate. Economic and political restructuring are required in addition to all those scientific approximations. And contemplative truth and interpersonal truth are likewise needed for any specifically structuring of a human society to make that society workable for humans and for the other life forms in this expanded industrial era.

We are currently challenged to consider how we make workable our phasing out of the massive fossil-fuel energizing of human society and phasing in an energizing that captures enough direct sun energy to power an industrial era society. The truth here includes what works to get this done. And this includes culture building, economic reorganizing, and the political action that keeps this going and curtails regression. This test of social workability is testing a fourth approach to truth that is different from the scientific, contemplative, and interpersonal approaches to truth and their tests for their truths. We continue to need all four types of approximate truths for operating a workable human society.

Neglecting any one of these four approaches to approximate truth weakens both human society and personal life. The overemphasis of individualism in current Western cultures tempts us neglect the commonalties of our cultural, political, and economic processes. We are response-able for our social commonalities, a service we neglect to our peril.

The Wholeness of our Our Fourfold-Approximation of Truth

All four of these approaches to truth are seeking truth about aspects of the same Profound Reality that is being encountered by us humans as *One Whole* unfoldment of our destiny. We do not confront four different overall realities—just One Reality in four different ways. We confront only one overall space/time flow of That Final Mystery about which we have our four forms of useful approximations.

In spite of this "final ignorance" in the life of the human species, we do, however, have our four different minds of approximate truth. These four distinct formulations of rational truth cannot be melded into one of them or rationally deduced from one of the four types of truth. We best opt to share in discovering and living all four of these truth quests. Truth for a human being is stored into four different human memory banks, and these four approaches to truth remain in a type of rational conflict with each another.

The human discipline of philosophy has the cultural task of creating practical whole views of thoughtfulness for the living of our historical destiny in the most effective and complete ways. The above briefly described *four-minded-ness* is an example of the sort of philosophizing that looks this irrationality in the face. I am claiming, along with others, that this *four-minded-ness* **is** built-into our human rationality that continues to be an aspect of the finite nature of the human mind as well as a quality for all our philosophical thoughtfulness. Pointing this out is good philosophy. This lack of hope for ever possessing one "theory of everything" that overcomes this four-foldedness of human truth will continue to be a frustration for some thoughtful people. Some strive to make science bear the whole load of truth. Others strive to make contemplative inquiry of subjectivity bear the whole load of truth. I am convinced that seeing the four-foldedness of human thoughtfulness makes for the very best philosophizing. It is my aim in this book to do such philosophizing in preparation for dong better religious theoretics, or theologizing.

If you need a professional philosopher to help you further understand this four-foldedness, I recommend Ken Wilber.[4] I have attempted to simplify much of what I have learned from Wilber. Wilber's complex writings have been a source of inspiration to me; nevertheless I am using my own language, with enrichments from A. H. Almaas, and decades of both scientific and religious study. Count me, not Wilber, responsible for these spins. Yet, I want to see philosophy in general make headway along these lines toward a better understanding of our human situation of approximate knowing within this Land of Mystery and in the light of our final ignorance as human beings.

---

[4] See Wilber, *Brief History of Everything*, 107

INTERFACING THE 7 LAYERS OF SECTION A WITH THE 4 APPROACHES OF SECTION B

IN SECTION C OF PART One, I am turning to some further expanding of the meaning of both the seven layers of natural intelligence and the four approaches to truth. This interfacing is pictured in the following chart (see next page). I will be discussing briefly each of the boxes of this chart. Section C will be divided into two subparts: (1) a short spin on columns 1, 2, & 3, Survival, Sensuality, and Purpose. I will call that section "From Algae and Amoeba to Fish." And (2) a subsection on columns 4, 5, 6, & 7. I will call that subsection "Mammals to Humans."

These reflections will describe a developmental story for each of our four approaches to truth within this One Land of Mystery. The *manyness* of evolving life gives us a fuller glimpse into the *Oneness* of the Profound Reality we find rushing toward us at the speed of time, always requiring of us fresh responses with our response ability, sometimes called "freedom."

SEVEN LAYERS OF NATURAL INTELLIGENCE IN THE HUMAM SPECIES

1 Survival	2 Sensuality	3 Purpose	4 Emotion	5 Symbolism	6 Intuition	7 Wonder	FOUR TYPES OF HUMAN KNOWING
All Life — Empulse for life Expansion	Animals — Pain, Pleasure, Sexuality	Complex Animals — Memory & Anticipation	Mammalian Animals — Bonding Relations	Human Animals — Language, Art, & Math	Beyond Symbols — 3rd Ear or 3rd Eye	the Awesome & the Awe — Trust, Care. & Freedom	
Rooted Living — Genetic Habits	Mobile Living — Enviromental Habits	Taking-in Surroudings — Complex Learning	Objectivity Distinguished from Subjectivity	Symbol Using & Abstraction skills	Paradigm Shift Capacities	Seeing the Limits of Scientific Truth	the scientific approach to truth
	Awareness of Pain & Pleasure	Awareness of Multi-sensory Reruns	Awarenes of Feeling & of Subjectivity Itself	Expressive Arts & Inward Inquiry	Silence & the Escape from Reason	The Invention of Religious Practices	the contemplative approach to truth
		Species Identification & Teamwork Arrangement	Bonding with the Living & Connecting with the Inanimate	The Development of Symbol-using Friendships	The Development of Therapy	The Meeting of Soul Mates	the interpersonal approach to truth
			Pre-Cultural Peer Groupings	The Origins of Human Culture	The Discovery of Cultural Relativity	The Activism of Perpetual Revolution	the commonality approach to truth

Sub-section 1: From Algae and Amoeba to Fish

Columns 1, 2, and 3 of the above chart

Our evolution begins 3.5 billion years ago in those murky first living cells. Something like an early algae was ancestor to the plants. Some one-celled creature like an Amoeba that could move around was ancestor to the animals. Here is a quotation that struck me about our early origins:

> You and the tree in your back yard come from a common ancestor. A billion and a half years ago, the two of you parted ways. But even now, after an immense journey in separate directions, that tree and you still share a quarter of your genes. [5]

The chakra-one foundations of human intelligence is a wisdom built into our bodies as well as into the trees. Chakra 1 intelligence has to do with an inherent drive and capacity to survive. I have noted that survival intelligence in column 1 of the above chart.

Chakra 2 and Column 2 of the above chart is about mobile life forms or animals that required sensualities for finding their way around in the environment. These pain and pleasure sensualities plus the intelligence to interpret the meanings of those environmental signals help these organisms to find safety and food as well as replicate their species and quite often spawn new species.

Column 3 and the chakra-3 life-dynamics pictured on the chart came into being, I am guessing, along with the multicellular life that characterized the more complex animals. These still early creatures required a capacity for memory and anticipation, an intelligence built

---

[5] Powers, Overstory, 445. This quotation comes from a novel, but the science behind these poetic words is correct.

with multi-sensory reruns and some storage and recall capacities for learning best case responses. I am viewing this process as the earliest roots of the more recent human highly-developed scientific approach to truth. And if these very early animals had any interior awareness of themselves, we can also guess that these were very earliest forms of our human capacities for the contemplative approach to truth. In the chart above I symbolized such very early internal awareness with the words "awareness of multi-sensory reruns." Similarly, I am describing these very earliest hints of interpersonal relations with the words "species identification" and "teamwork arrangement."

These very early chakra 1, 2, and 3 chakra developments are my guesses based on what very little we actually know about these early developments of life on Earth.

Subsection 2: Mammals to Humans

Columns 4, 5, 6, & 7 of the above chart

Much more and better data guides my guesses for the writing of subsection 2 of the above chart, for this subsection develops a picture of the evolving of each of the four types of knowing in relation to the general development from mammalian to human types of intelligence already introduced in Part One A with a general description of chakras 4, 5, 6, & 7.

Mammals are characterized by a much further development than the reptiles and birds with respect to a much more powerful emotional intelligence—chakra 4—equipping mammals with a deeper knowledge of themselves and other species as well as capacities for caring more carefully for their young. These emotional gifts have also enabled the mammals to share emotional bonds with humans who are, of course, also mammals—primates with an expansion of intelligence into three more chakra levels of intelligence—5, 6, & 7.

I will divide this 2nd subsection of Section C into these four topics: the four rows of the above chart in dialogue with the last four chakra columns—Emotion, Symbols, Intuition, & Wonder. Here are the titles of the four topics:

1. The Development of Scientific Intelligence
2. The Development of Contemplative Intelligence
3. The Development of Interpersonal Intelligence
4. The Development of Commonality Intelligence

1. The Development of Scientific Intelligence

I begin my discussion of Subsection 2 of Section C of Part One with reflections on the scientific approach to the truth in relations with these four chakra levels of natural intelligence 4, 5, 6, and 7. I will do so in a developmental manner—describing the evolution and intensification of awareness and freedom and the social forms of the scientific approach to approximate truth.

As we in the West customarily use the term "science," the scientific approach to truth begins in human history a century or two before Aristotle with names like Pythagoras. But the origins of science can be viewed as earlier than that and more widespread than the ancient Athenian luminaries of the scientific approach to truth.

Perhaps we can date the origin of the scientific approach to truth with the dawn of language and mathematics. That may have occurred at least as early as 30,000 years ago where we find in France those remarkable caves of art done by out-of-Africa migrants of our current species. I am suggesting that we define the birth of science as whenever it was that humans first began testing the validity of their mental projects of thought with their collected objective experiences of their senses. Also, we can imagine precursors to the human form of scientific thinking in earlier mammalian species who were using their remembered images of multi-sensory reruns rather than our uniquely human mental entitles that we are calling "symbols."

I have already illustrated the meaning of "symbols" as a mental entity used in the processes we call "language," "art", and "mathematics." The development and use of symbols made a big difference from the species in whom the multi-sensory rerun mental entity was used exclusively . Humans share with the other animals this multi-sensory using intelligence, and they add to it their symbol using intelligence. The lack of symbol using in our dogs and cats and horses, does not prevent these fellow mammalian species from being "scientific" in their more limited ways.

For example, when a dog finds a human body buried in the snow, a form of thoughtfulness is at work that is at least science-like. This sort of pre-human "thinking" might date back in origin earlier than the mammals, but I will not speculate further about how those pre-mammalian species think. Yet perhaps all animal life, being mobile rather than rooted like plants and fungi, has needed a science-like intelligence that plants and fungi do not need.

While our human consciousness of being conscious of consciousness was surely not present in the early period of mammalian life before there were primates, we can suppose that a level of consciousness is present in all mammals that store emotional wisdom and chose how to use that wisdom to optimize their living. This awareness of inward emotion surely have enabled an increased distinction of objective from subjective. I will say no more about these deep roots of science. I will start my detailed discussion on the origin of the scientific approach to truth in the row of boxes on the above chart where the scientific approach to truth intersects with a box in the column of the chart labeled "4. Emotion." This box in the chart is named "Objectivity Distinguished from Subjectivity."

Objectivity Distinguished from Subjectivity

I am assuming that the development of what we now describe as the emotional intelligence of humans began with the origin of the mammals. All mammals, including humans have the benefits of this powerful ability to make emotional connections with our mates, our young, our teammates, and other species companions. We humans and other mammals conduct bonding not only with our fellow living creatures but also with inanimate objects, places, and times.

This means that we mammals have more awareness of our subjectivity or inwardness than the earlier forms of animal life. Mammals distinguished themselves from the lives of the reptiles, dinosaurs, and birds with this expanded emotional intelligence. This greater awareness of inwardness also meant a greater awareness of objectivity, for it can be assumed that pre-mammalian animal life could make little or no differentiation between inward and outward reality. These earlier evolved forms of life experienced sensations of pain, pleasure and other feelings, but in their awareness of Reality, I am assuming, they did not and still do not distinguish these sensations as inward or objective or store them into separate memory cabinets. So let us theorize that for the most part the forms of life that were earlier in origin than the mammals were making no or very little distinction between inward and outward. Those two parts of all conscious experience came mixed together into one memory stored in one way.. Therefore, no foundation was laid for the awareness of a thoroughgoing objectivity that was needed for a development of the scientific approach to truth in the human form. For the fish, alligators, turtles, and snakes encounters come as a blend of inward and outward aspects with no awareness (or extremely little) with which to distinguish objective from subjective.

Some might assume that this lack of distinction was an advantage, for the outward and the inward realism do come as one reality. Some humans like to say that subjectivity is just an objective part of life. Other humans like to say that only subjectivity is real, the objective view is illusory. But the objective view is essential to science. And subjectivity taken by itself would be a limitation on truth as much as objectivity taking by itself. Here is a ready illustration of truth that subjectivity alone, however intense, could never have come uncovered. Those big bones found in the ground reveal the existence of the dinosaurs some 65 millions years ago on this planet. The contemplative inquiry into subjectivity cannot do away with the realism of science any more than science can be a replacement for the contemplative inquiry into subjectivity, Humans do both. Reptiles do neither. Mammals other than humans are a transition.

Symbol-using and Abstraction Skills

Though the early forms of mammalian life appeared about 200,000,000 years ago, we can choose, if we like, to limit our human definition of the scientific approach to truth with the development of language, art, and mathematics in the homosapien species. This still makes science over 30,000 years old, a solid structure of living that no fully functioning modern human would be wise to be without. Seeing even a 15,000 year old antiquity for science assumes that science is at its roots concerned with anticipating the future of objective events in order to make decisions in the present that optimize species living.

Natural science, as summarized by Aristotle (384-322 BCE), has had a long run with many add-ons and transformations, such as the amazing work of Sir Isaac Newton. What happened to our view of the scientific approach to truth through the paradigm shifts of Einstein and the explorations of quantum mechanics needs further comment to fully illuminate the nature of science.

The Nobel Prize winning physicist Richard Feynman summarized the essence of the scientific method as follows. This is my summation: You guess a new theory in terms of the facts you know and the possibilities you don't know and then you create an experiment that can test the validity of your guess. If the test fails you guess again. If the test succeeds you have a new functional law of nature until tests of that new theory do fail the tests of observation. In the next box of my chart, I will attempt to describe briefly the interface of the scientific approach to truth with the natural intelligence qualities of chakra 6. This next box is about the role of *intuition* in the nature of scientific work.

Paradigm Shift Capacities

Using the concept of "paradigm," scientific philosophers begun discussing more deeply the role of intuition at work in the careers of our edge scientists. For example, how does a scientist's mind move from a universe-wide view like Newton's physics to an alternative universe-wide view like Einstein's physics. To make such a shift is like moving into a significantly different universe, for almost none of the basic ideas remain unchanged. Let us try to imagine the mind of such a scientist creating a shift between what *was* for a time "reasonable" into a whole *new* mode of what *is* "reasonable." There is a gap of chaos between these two modes of "reasonable." If we imagine living for a time in this gap of sheer imagination, we can experience the natural intelligence of intuition.

Though such a scientist is following the clues of the objective facts and how current fact-descriptions are supporting or not supporting current physical understandings, a whole new paradigm of understanding is an act of creation out of nothing by the powers of human imagination itself. This awareness has given to our most inclusive thinkers a new sense of the truth that all scientific knowledge is vulnerable to very deep changes. An entire system of scientific thought can go to pieces, so to speak, and be replaced by a truth that was never thought before.

Looking backward from our post-Newton-to-now-Einstinian paradigm shift we can see that paradigm shifting is a much older experience. We see an example of paradigm shifting in the story of Copernicus and his solar-rotations view. A spherical planet was a big challenge to the flat-Earth view that was still held by most of Copernicus' society. Notice how these circles or ellipses around the sun have become the common sense of culture because they fit more accurately to the actual facts of the physical world. A paradigm shift is more than an arbitrary way of seeing things. It means living in a whole new universe of humanely perceived realism.

Science now continues its perpetual changes within the awareness that new paradigms of understanding are commonly possible. Powerful resting places will be reached, but they are all plateaus. This mountain of scientific understanding has no top. The more we know, the more we know that we don't know. A scientific research to end the unknown only opens up the unknown into a wider scope. We can, however, have better scientific approximations of the real world. We know is is better because let gives order where a previous paradigm failed to do so.

Seeing the Limits of Scientific Truth

The lead edges of scientific-thinking and philosophizing in our contemporary world has discovered that not only is scientific thought vulnerable to paradigm shifts, it is also true that the scientific approach to truth has always been and always will be only one among four quite different approaches to approximating the truth of this Awesome Land of Mystery in which we all live. This now increasingly clear awareness asks us to give up the notion that there is a comprehensive view of truth that the scientific approach to truth can encompass.. While some scientists and others still hope for a cause-and-effect wholeness (or at least a probability type of wholeness) created by science alone, our actual experience of the One and Only Land of Mystery of Profound Reality is teaching us to see otherwise. All truth of any sort is about approximating The Truth of that Whole of what is Real. This awareness is not an anti-science view. We are all scientists and need to be, but our science and anyone's science is limited knowledge—limited by the further reaches of human knowledge-seeking itself.

2. The Development of Contemplative Intelligence

The human truth seeking that I have called "contemplative inquiry" includes a path to understanding contained in good art and all the humanities as well as the truth sought and found through lasting religious practices such as meditation, subjective inquiry, theologizing, and more. We also find our contemplative intelligences a topic in our most sensitive biologies, in our depth psychologies and in our interpersonal psychologies, and in our existential philosophies and existential histories. It is fair to say that our contemplative means of human thoughtfulness balance in life importance with our scientific thoughtfulness. Subjectivity is as real as the sensorial objectivity that is sought by the sciences.

What is objective to our own bodies and what is the subjectively experienced within our own bodies are part of the same overall

Reality, but strict science limits its test for truth to objective inputs. The subjective scope is known to the scientist, but for truth testing a research scientist is silent about his subjective tests for truth. How I, as scientist, feel or what I want has no place in determining the speed of light or the strength needs of a bridge girder. The scientist does employ his subjective imagination in designing theories, nevertheless, the test of the truth of a scientific theory is only objective in the outward nature of our environment. Subjective truth requires a different type of inquiry.

The subjective experiences of the human is a wide realm of experience and of thoughtfulness that can be applied to our inward experience. The data of contemplative inquiry, however, cannot properly be called "objective facts," but something different. Let us call these data "contemplative phenomena." The objective scientist can deal with the sounds, reports, and behaviors of living beings, but "contemplative phenomena" are not part of a scientific proof, even if the scientific theory under question is about the inner world of experiences.

We simply have two realms of rational truth, and the concepts of each rational realm do not always match. For example, "time" in the scientific mode of truth is pictured as a line separating past from future with the infinitesimal point labeled "now." But in the contemplative approach to truth, "time" is always and only "now." The past is only memory in the now. And the future is only an anticipation in the now. Time is a flow through the now-body of the contemplating human.

Every human being is a contemplative, as well as a scientist. Different persons and cultures may lean one way or other in their emphasis, but our species is characterized by two equivalent intellectual powers—each means of truth interpreting the other in their own context. The contemplative approach can views science as producing abstract worlds that are somewhat useful for predicting the real future. The scientist is simply silent about our subjective realm in the scientific test for truth.

The boxes in the contemplation row of the above chart are interfaced with chakra 4, 5, 6, and 7 of our human body-based natural intelligence. Those who work with horses often notice a very powerful emotionality that we humans share with other mammalian species. The box that occurs at the intersection of chakra 4 and the contemplative approach to truth is an attempt to describe the nature of that form of contemplative inquiry we share with the horse or dog or cat with whom we may live. That box on the contemplative row of the above chart I have entitled "awareness of subjectivity." Let us notice that we can experience a cat as aware of "my" subjectivity as well as "I" of the cat's subjectivity.

Awareness of Subjectivity

Under this title, I summarize my intuitions of the mammalian qualities of awareness that preceded the development the symbol-using human form of contemplative inquiry. This box is about aspects of the mammalian form of natural intelligence that humans share with the other mammals, most prominently with the other primates. We sometimes call this our "emotional intelligence." This "awareness of subjectivity," is featured, we intuit, in mammalian emotionality, is a deeper consciousness than we find among the reptiles. A deeper awareness of subjectivity is found in mammals that is not found in pre-mammalian forms of life.

So, I am guessing that the degree of consciousness needed for making a clear distinction concerning an inner life has not yet dawned in these earlier originated life forms. Such emotionality is dawning in the early mammals and flourishing in the primates.. And it has quite fully dawned in human beings. This is true even though so many of we humans employ our symbol using skills to suppress our emotions. Mammalian emotionality remains strong in our humanity and with it we have an awareness of subjectivity and that makes possible an inward inquiry that is of great importance for human life.

Expressive Arts & Inward inquiry

In the human species a strong inward aliveness has definitely taken on expressions with the various forms of art. We can guess that at least sculpture, dance, elemental toning, and the rhythm aspects of music came into play along with language— perhaps earlier than language. We have in the archeological record very early sculptures and flute instruments. We have cave paintings in France that date back 30,000 years and suggest an even earlier existence than that for paintings. The linguistic arts of song, poetry, story, drama, and novel came into being after language got underway. Architecture as an art was still later. Music in its current complex forms of notation and composition is also a later innovation. These rough historical overviews indicates that art and language came into being alongside one another. The bone fragments of the homo-erectus skulls indicate that the larynx of these upright-walking primates were not yet able to do complex speech, even though other means of communication were probably well developed. The development of linguistic speech with sentence structure is surly only present after 100,000 years ago as the homo species developed a different larynx. The non-linguistic arts such as sculpture, painting, music, and dance may have preceded the full development of language. Mathematics is also very old in its simpler forms, but not likely as old as the simple forms of language. In summary, I am using the term "expressive arts" to indicate the richness of a very early stage in the life of that symbol-using species we call "human."

Silence and the Escape from Reason

When the contemplative approach to truth intersects with the intuitional level of our natural intelligence (chakra 6), I am suggesting some strong third-eye or a third-ear experiences in art making, as well as a "seeing" of visions or a "hearing" of voices where ordinary sight and hearing, as well as ordinary language and mathematics are blind and deaf. "Intuition" points to a real interior awareness. "Silence" is a word used to characterize some of these states of awareness. The noise and pictures of the mind can be escaped into a "inner space" of silence. Here is a phrase of poetry I like: "I climb out of the river of thought and sit by the bank listening"—listening to the flowing river of both thought and senses." The reasoning to which we cling and with which we attempt to control life can be stilled for a moment. This escape from our busy minds does not mean that the mind quits functioning; it means that our mental function is being demoted from being our whole consciousness of Reality. Our experiences of silence can be seen as holding all mental processing at arm length, so to speak—seeing our reasoning from the point of view of a spaciousness of awareness that includes rationality rather than of being contained within rationality.

We still live within a culture of human creations and within our own lifetime of thoughtfulness, but we also occupy a spaciousness of awareness that can make us an outsider from our culture—even an outsider to our own life history. This is not something supernatural or spooky. Our genuine history-changing human creativity comes from this place of spaciousness. It is from this "spaciousness" that we can speak of choices that are "creations out of nothing."

This spaciousness of Mysterious Reality can also be known as a Nothingness out of which our free choices are made and from which new cultural aspects are created. "Spaciousness" is a symbolic "place" from which our truly free spontaneity of life is constructed. This spaciousness is a relation to our busy mind that does not actually stop our busy mind from being busy. It is our essential consciousness or awareness that discovers this stillness, this silence, this creativity out of which "nowhere land" we can create anew more expanded mental worlds in which we then proceed to carry on in our practical everyday living. This creativity is a type of awakening in the evolution of our species, and our making of these escapes from old reasoning are very old. We can guess that these spaciousness awakenings have been taking place for humans for at least 30,000 years.

The Invention of Religious Practices

Wonder or awe before the awesomeness of Profound Reality is a state of contemplative awareness. And wonder is a birth within our natural intelligence with which we are made capable of inventing religious practices that assist us to experience this profoundness. This proficiency then assists us to assist others to allow their lives to be filled by the Awesome Overallness with the awe or wonder of the omnipresent Awesomeness of ever-present Profoundness of Reality. Herein we unearth the deepest levels of the contemplative approach to truth.

The states of consciousness we are talking about in this regard are aspects of our ordinary natural intelligence—a provoking of that natural intelligence to its fastest spin, so to speak. It is these states of profound consciousness that can invent the effective symbolic icons, dances, stories, and methods that give expression to our experiences of Profound Reality and thereby qualify to be called "religion." There are, of course, many instances of obsolete and corrupted "religion" that tarnish the deepest meanings of the word. "religion." I will insist that this is the tarnishing of a good thing in the way that bad economics is also a tarnishing of a good thing. Just as we do not dismiss economics because so much of it is bad, we do not need to dismiss religious because so much of it is bad.

And I will insist that all religion is a temporal thing created by temporal human beings. No religion has dropped down from heaven or risen up from Earth to be the complete pattern of a final authority. It is only Profound Reality that is truly profound. Our profound consciousness of Profound Reality is simply a temporal part of our ordinary experience when we are experiencing Profound Reality consciously. Religious practices are human creations adapted to a particular temporal human society for the sake of making our human awareness of Profound Reality more likely. Such useful religious practices are very old. Long before there were civilizations, their were religious practices.

I am going to explore examples of these very old religious creations in Part Two of this book. I end this introduction to the evolution of contemplative inquiry with this statement: *we now live in a massive planet-wide contemplative awakenment of awareness of Profound Reality that will continue to spawn religious renewals and religious creations.*

3. The Development of Interpersonal Intelligence

I am now moving to the third row of the last four columns of the above chart . The development of our interpersonal savvy begins as soon as we are born. Before we have the reflective skills to think about our interpersonal relations, we are deep into the process of interpersonal learning. For her survival, the human infant must be nestled into a set of interpersonal relations that begin layer-after-layer of natural and social savvy. Interpersonal intelligence has very old roots in pre-human mammalian living. On my chart above, I label the first box on the interpersonal row as "Species Identification & Teamwork Arrangements." I am suggesting with this box title that reptiles, dinosaurs, and birds also have an interpersonal intelligence, and that intelligence is then enriched by the evolution of mammalian emotionality. I will begin my description of the development of interpersonal intelligence with this box on mammalian interpersonal life as it is emerging in the interpersonal row.

Bonding with the Living; Connecting with the Inanimate

Hundred of millions of years before the dawn of the human mode of consciousness, mammalian life evolved a powerful emotional intelligence for bonding with its young, its own species, some other species, even inanimate objects and places. Cows, I understand, have best friends. Cats, dogs, horses, and other mammals can bond strongly with humans. We can surmise that such emotionally intense relationships occurred among mammals long before the human development of dance, music, ritual, language, song, poetry, icon, myth, sculpture, story, mathematics, drama, architecture, temples, urban planning, and so on. The interpersonal qualities inherited from the earlier mammalian evolution, especially from earlier primates, were foundational for the interpersonal lives of humans, and humans have enhanced these foundations by the unique capacities the human species. But long before there were humans, there were creatures on this planet who bonded with the living and connected with their environments emotionally.

The Development of Symbol-using Friendships

Human friendships, matings, and cooperative actions using language, art, and mathematics gave interpersonal relationships an enhanced quality over the earlier hominids and apes. We humans begin early in our lives building conscious interpersonal ties, bonds, and cooperations. By adulthood, a savvy human has typically developed the interpersonal approach to truth to a deep level—even though many humans suppress their emotional and interpersonal capacities.

By "symbol-using" friendships" I mean the importance among humans that is given to talking with each other, thinking together, planning together, organizing into teams of planning, action, and more. Touch is a factor. Sex is a factor. Conscious presence is a factor. And thoughtfulness is a factor. The evolution of the capacities for symbol-using friendships is an enormous enhancement of human living,—a large realm both for another layer of suffering and for another layer of optimized living.

The Development of Therapy

I am using the word "therapy" as a symbol for the development within interpersonal relations for using our third ear or third eye type of intelligence that is described in the chakra 6 layer of natural intelligence for the healing of estrangements, confusions, stuck places, and more.. In other words, "therapy" means having the *intuition* to see beyond the skills of using language, art, and mathematics and to move toward still deeper places from which to build the stories, customs, and principles to guide our living.

The chakra 6 level of awareness and freedom enables humans with the skills of sensing the consciousness of consciousness presence within one's own self and within the conscious life of other humans. This therapeutic presence also includes the skill of sensing unconsciousness and lying. This layer of consciousness is not the emotionality of chakra 4, nor is it the wisdom of chakra 5's thoughtful advise. Therapy is a quality of interpersonal living that has been advanced for thousands of years by shaman, priests, story tellers, and best friends.

This layer of consciousness is best understood as a consciousness of consciousness operating for the healing of consciousness among other human beings. I am also describing that layer of natural intelligence as it applies to a successful interpersonal relationship within which each person is serving the other with truth, rather than promoting their ego-imaginations and their favorite lies. The very presence of truth expression is movement toward therapeutic healing. Therapy is a discussion that rescues the human from wrong turns into illusion and dead ends we don't easily change.

We can surmise from our minimum knowledge of hunter/gatherer societies that the *shaman* who were prominent within these societies were of therapeutic service to others within those early successful societies. I am guessing that many of these shaman were playing a useful role in assisting persons to adapt to the enigmatic environments of nature and human sociality.. We can imagine that these rather small and parochial societies could be psychologically fragile and in dire need of the services of these shaman. Without some capacity to ground the inner life of a population in solid realism, an entire primitive society could pass away in forms of psychosis. We can surely thank those hundreds of thousands of years of creative shaman for adapting human living to some of our most basic patterns of sanity.

The Meeting of Soul-Mates

"Soul mates" will be my symbol for the experience of meeting another human being on the profound consciousness level of awareness and freedom. This chakra 7 level of interpersonal life is about sharing awe or wonder. "Soul mates" is a term that is often used for relationships less profound than this—such as a strong emotional and/or sensual/sexual bonding. Such mammalian types of meeting are wholesome parts of our interpersonal life, but I want to reserve the poetry of "soul mates" for a deeper type of interpersonal meeting.

A chakra 7 soul mate can be between two men or two women as well a man and a woman. Sexual attraction and sexual practice may or may not also be involved. Describing this type of interpersonal richness is difficult, for describing chakra 7 levels of consciousness is difficult. The words "wonder" and "awe" can be useful if we do not trivialize these words into the sort of meanings we sometimes express with phases like "my awesome automobile." An openness to wonder and acting from wonder requires a stretching of ordinary language into metaphorical expressions—that deep sort of poetry that these "soul-mates" understand together.

In this box of the above chart, I also want to alert us to interpersonal relations among groups of people who are experiencing characteristics similar to the Pentecost happening as described by Luke in his Acts of the Apostles. This Pentecost group of people did not even speak the same language. At this Jesus memorial, they had no need for words to recognize one another as participants in an ecstatic consciousness that was sweeping over them—a deeply awesome wonder in the midst of some fresh reckoning with Profound Reality. They did not know what to call it, so Peter suggested "the resurrection of Messiah Jesus." Later others Christian interceptors called this "Holy Spirit."

4. The Development of Commonality Intelligence

We are now looking at the fourth row of the above chart. The intelligence of commonality practices develops in the story of human life after the dawn of art, language, and mathematics—also after the development of the objective memory of science, the subjective memory of contemplation, and a third memory bank of interpersonal savvy it requires for teams of thinking persons to live intimately and work effectively together.

The commonality of human societies is built on the framework of societal practice evolved in the pre-human mammalian species, but it is not correct to lump the nature of human communal life with that of the other mammalian species. What we humans are describing with the commonality possible for the human species differs greatly from other living species. These pre-human gatherings and cooperations do give to the human adventure a sort of foundation for their economic, political and cultural life. Team defenses and team food finding is foundational for human living, but the addition of the human gifts of language, art, and mathematics transform almost everything about a human society from the society of the chimpanzees and other apes. Nevertheless, I will again begin my story of the development of human commonality intelligence with elements from the social life of pre-human mammals.

Pre-cultural Peer Groupings

Food gathering-and-catching, food distribution among adults and babies, and some tool making reached a high decree of development among upright walking primates before the dawn of art, language, and mathematics. These developments among pre-human mammals, however, must not be termed an economic system of the homosapien sort. Nevertheless, the economic life of these mammals were foundations for the economic systems of homo-sapiens that blossomed after the birth of human culture. Something similar can be said about human political systems. This pre-cultural peer group of pre-human primate life accomplished with their multi-sensory rerun type of thoughtfulness (chakra 3 and 4 intelligence), a useful social life that had its political-like aspects. Nevertheless, let us remain open to discern the vast differences in commonality creations and histories that are enabled by the symbol using capacities of the chakra-5 humans. A human society uses the gift of language to work out its political arrangements, assignments, and decision-making processes. Both human economic processes and human political processes require the processes of a human culture—a life of art, language, and mathematics to use in sharing our experiences of being consciousness beings working together to optimize our lives—both our personal lives and our social lives of human-made, social environments.

The Origins of Human Culture

The exact motive for and the order of the events that led to the origins of human cultures are largely invisible in the archeological records, The time-gap in which this evolutionary development took place may have begun as early as the expanding brain size of the homo species that began around 200,000 years ago. Much cultural know how must have been established by the time of the presence of the advanced art in those 30,000-year-old caves in France. We have a 60,000-year-old Neanderthal flute with four pierced holes. made from the left thighbone of a young cave bear. We have a few caved objects of artistic and/ or religious import created slightly before 30,000 years ago. Dances, rituals, and icons of wood of those early years are not now visible. Nevertheless, we can assume some sort of slow step-by-step evolution of language, art, and mathematics, emerged at the same time that the brain size of the homo species expanded. And with that expansion and its symbol using, a human culture emerged.

Some researchers have discovered that these 30,000 year old

paintings were in caves that were also acoustical chambers compared with the other such caves where paintings were not present. So we archeologist inclined humans can speculate that singing was done and music was played in those art-decorated caves. These places may have served as "cathedrals" in which awe inspiring practices were conducted. We do not know how much earlier such things took place. It may be that forms of religion practice were in being much earlier.

We can guess that mathematics is later in development than art, language, and religion. The logic within language is a form of mathematics, but mathematics might be defined as a much more extensive exploration of the abstract ordering capacities of the symbol-using human mind. As to the origin of language itself, I was struck by some lessons I took from a Native American on toning. In this course we learned to communicate with only vowel sounds in song creations of all sorts. It seems likely to me that humans may have became competent in the use of such sounding to one another long before we became capable of using carefully distinguish sounds abstractly for quick communications and also developing the syntax-type ordering of words we call "sentences."

Along with the origins of a human manner of cultural processes based on the use of language, art, mathematics and religious symbolizing, we also had the origin of a human manner of economic processing that was based on the interactions of being a symbol-using group of thoughtful people who were also mammalian animals requiring food and shelter and other Earth-bound resources. These processes already had their foundations in the life-ways of the pre-human-upright-walking primates, but as we have developed through human history the life-ways of a homosapien-type of economics, we have found ourselves envisioning these human economic life ways in three basic groupings: (1) the accessing of Earth *resources* (2) the *producing* of useful-to-humans products and services, and (3) the *distribution* to one another of those socially produced items and services.

A similar development in *political* processes took place along with our symbol-using *cultural* processes, and our symbol-using *economic* processes. All upright-walking primates of the homo-big-brained type were using fire, making complex tools, hunting together, gathering together and thereby developing some sort of political-like processes that were more human-like than like than those of the smaller-brained chimpanzee-like common ancestors.

Language, art, mathematics, and religion made a big differences in what political process became in the life of the homosapien species. More complex *decision-making* processes had to be developed. *Geographical scopes* for hunting-& gathering and later national boundaries had to be rationally defined. And the exercise of *social power* through norms, customs, laws, and enforcements had to be designed. By who and how social decisions are made, forms a third aspect of human political processes.

We symbol-using humans developed a range of *cultural* processes well beyond the pre-symbol-using animal skills already described. *Common Sense* processes emerged as: (1) basic disciplines of learning preserved and improved from generation to generation, (2) useful methods of doing things that were then taught, and passed along from generation to generation, and (3) *institutions of education and information sharing* of ever-more-complex types.

Still further defining the meaning of *Cultural Processes* are *Common Style* processes, including: (1) roles for women, for men, for youth, for elders, etc. (2) modes of association, (3) taboos, moral patterns, assumptions for peaceful life together and for conflict resolutions. Each human culture consists of specific symbol-using processes; Art, language, and religions being primary. The complexity and diversity of all these social processes appears to know no bounds. Nevertheless, some basic architecture of essential human social processes can be described and the relations among these various social processes also described.

The Discovery of Cultural Relativity

I am racing the clock forward to our period with industrial civilization from our hunter-gatherer period through a pre-civilization period that included agriculture and other complexities, and on to the those first civilizational hierarchies and city centered societies. We are now discovering the rather shocking truths of cultural relativity. Rather than viewing our cultural environments as simply part of nature or perhaps given to our group of humans by some everlasting gods and goddesses, we are discovering the obvious truth that each cultural tradition was hand-made by its human ancestors and continues to be arbitrarily re-designed by existing human beings.

In modern times we humans are living together on one planet. We have bumped into very different alien cultures so forcefully that we have coined the term "cultural shock." We have discovered how deeply we are formed into the mold of a given cultural development, and how unwilling we can be to see reality through any other cultural eyes than our own. Cultural relativity is not only about taking in the strangeness of other cultures of people, but also about taking in the limitations, lacks, and issues of our own home culture. Opening ourselves to these deep truths means confronting and curtailing our outlandish cultural bigotries, our put-downs of other cultures, and our violences toward peoples different from our own arbitrary and limited social conditioning.

The relativity or our home culture and of all other cultures is not a small discovery about our humanity. It has vast implications for our future. We can now become vividly aware that no matter how advanced we may view our culture, there is much yet to learn from all those other cultural sources.

The dialogue between what we have called East and West has become electrifyingly, horrifying, and enriching for both sides of this exchange of vastly different forms of religions, art, life style, ways of organizing, novel patterns of association, etc. The horrific alienations between African and European cultures are beginning to thaw. In places where these two types of cultures have been forced to live together, often under grim circumstances of white oppression, these deeply different gifts have nevertheless been exchanged and done so in ways that enriched both cultures.

Another dialogue of oppressive quality has begun to thaw between European and Native American cultures. Many other dialogues are taking place with many different levels of trauma. This stew of peoples is expanding our realization of our humanity, however painful this has been and still is being and becoming. This pain is rooted in our clinging to the cultures we know and resisting other learnings, often to the extent of considering these various other cultures as non-human life ways, rather than as opportunities for the enrichment of our own cultural lives as well as the healing of long suffered twists and oppressions that our inherited cultural forms currently hold.

The Activism of Perpetual Revolution

The interaction of the commonality approach to truth with the seventh chakra of natural intelligence is the topic of this last box in my discussion of the above chart. Chakra 7 intelligence deals with states of awe that challenge all sorts of mental and cultural oppression. Hence these few following paragraphs will be a very incomplete summary of this complex and difficult topic. I will be exploring this topic more in the Part Two of this short book. Basically, we are dealing here with the interface of human social life with the inward events of awakenment, or enlightenment, or being rescued from fallenness, or being in awe by the encounters with Awesome Profound Reality, and still other ways of talking about the 7th chakra of natural intelligence in religion metaphors.

In addition, the topic of this box is the interface of these many states of profound awareness with the also complex and difficult to discuss commonality approach to truth. I have named this box "perpetual revolution" to indicate both the effect of charka seven on social life and the effect of this ever-changing social life on our discussion of charka 7 experiences.

The word "revolution" does not mean a full 360 degree twirl to the sociological status quo, but a 90 to 180 degree turn into some quite different directions from these taken-for-granted directions of the existing societies in which we humans are so deeply conditioned. Such revolutionary changes in our social forms are never ending in the sense of the never arriving of a final society. Apocalyptic visions of our social life can us be useful mythology if we do not let such visions degenerate into literal predictions or arrogant superstitions.

On planet Earth, there is actually no place of unchanging rest for our social organizations. Economic, political, snd cultural process all move into new forms and keep moving. For example, various versions of both capitalism and socialism are already way out of date. And we can also see efforts to learn from both of these heritages how to create "an economics as if Earth matters." Also our basic cultural relations can be created "as if human authenticity matters." Such workable directions are going to recommend forms of democracy that are often hated by most of the billionaire classes who feel their power and wealth is being eroded. Hatred of democracy also occurs in infuriated cults of obsolete culture and religion who find their "way of life" unraveling.

When "democratization" is what we are talking about, many of us are already opening to the awareness that we have only begun to know what a full democracy looks like. We can see, looking backward in U.S. history, that slaves were granted freedom and have been taking up strong forms of citizenship, and that women after winning the vote are now busy making immense improvements in the democracy that was started by those original male writers of the U.S. constitution. In this US nation practicing the early forms of democracy, we still do not assure a living wage to persons working 40 hours a week. We still do not assure women the unrestrained right to have control over their own bodies We still do not provide healthcare as a right for all persons. We still do not even assure all black persons of police protection, rather than police harassment and many untimely deaths at the hands of bigoted, frightened, power-hungry, and defensive police-persons who need to be forced to take up another employment. Democracy is a political commonality that is forever moving on against such status-quo arrangements. Democracy viewed in this perpetual-revolution context may still protect its accomplishments with a constitution and norms of practice, but, nevertheless, be a way of life that includes perpetual changes in the specified definitions of justice and workability of the overall society and its planet-wide democratic relations.

Finally, the underlying mix of cultures that make up most human societies today are also in perpetual revolution. This truth about approximate knowing can get lost in these complexities. Each culture is doing its own development, and each group of cultures is moving along together in many ways. Furthermore, for each move into a deeper realism, there is a reaction or retreat into ever more stubborn defenses of some status quo. In the midst of these quarrels, there can also arise fanatical reactionary retreats into this or that mis-remembered past. The way forward is never a set path of inevitable progress toward an already known greater realism, nor is there a set path moving into an inevitable regression into ever deeper delusions.

The key enduring factor is the human ability for continuing to make those hard decisions between realism and delusion. Good decisions have leaders, but they likewise have to be worked through within group decision-making from local to planetary levels. However challenging these considerations may be, real possibilities for greater realism do exist. Effective pathways can be found, but we humans have to find them. Such is the approximate knowledge within the commonality approach to truth lived at the 7th chakra level of human intelligence operation.

One last question needs to be answered before ending this quick summary of the deep development of the commonality approach to truth. How is realism, as opposed to delusion, to be discerned. Social workability can be our test for social realism. Social workability includes an honest application of the other three quests for truth. And "social workability" is a term for an additional test of truth. Some social arrangements lead to the disintegration of a given society. Some social arrangements lead to injustices that are so rank that the oppressed members will carry off a revolt that may do more harm than help. Laziness, foolishness, arrogance, individualistic overemphasis, collectivistic overemphasis, and more can lead to all sorts of social unworkability. Unworkability is the enemy of a deep practice of reality-loving responsibility for each human society,—correcting its past, preserving its present gifts, and inventing its future possibilities. Our current wisdom of social workability is an approximate knowledge in a quest for more social-workability. And our concepts of workability are also a sort of truth that remains approximate. Final answers to the commonality of human social life will never be found. Perpetual revolution is the only "game in town" for the pursuit of our more realistic and just human societies.

CONCLUSIONS TO PART ONE

the relativity of human identity

It has become misleading to say that I am a Christian, or that I am a Buddhist, or that I am a Muslim. I am far more than my religious practice. It might be more accurate to say that I practice a Muslim religion.—or that I practice a Jewish religion—or that I practice a Christian religion—or that I practice a Buddhist religion. But when human identity has been attached to a religious practice of any type, bigotry results, contempt of some sort is being spawned, some sort of oppression is arising, and war too often follows. Do we need examples that show this? Will the Palestinian conflict do? Will the conflicts in Ireland do? Will Hindus and Muslims in India do? Will Muslims and Christians in Spain do? The US also has its religious wars.

Or if I say "I am French," "I am German," "I am American," etc. this can also be a form of bigotry. The deep roots of human living that we are seeing today is that our human identity is a deeper issue than these various silos of political, economic, or cultural differences. There are endless ways of identifying ourselves with some factual but finite distinction, but all these distinctions are but roles we play—relative, penultimate differences rather than final identities for being human.

I am especially signaling the deep truth that our "religion" is just a practice of thinking and ritualizing and ethically doing. No religion, however useful in accessing experience of the Lasting Eternal Reality is itself anything eternal. So even these semi-sacred things cannot be an identity we must live and die for.

For example, Rudolf Bultmann, among others, discovered that the core of Christian faith is not a religious identity of any sort, but rather a "true deed" of trust in the trustworthiness of Profound Reality. Such an aggressive "faith" is a human choice. But I do not choose my human essence. I am given the possibility of choosing to trust the human essence that I am being giving in this moment and the next and the next moment of my life.

I tend to enter each given moment having opted to want to cling to some "better" past moment or to hope for some "better" future moment. To live this given moment fully means to treasure the gifts of its past as well as to welcome the possibilities of its future and to make my history-bending choices in this moment.

Remembered past and anticipated future are part of living the moment I am now given, and to living this moment in a full trust in the trustworthiness of the Profound Reality that is giving me this moment. Such laying back into such trusting of my Real Life can result in a life flowing with true bliss in spite of all its ups and downs. In order to cease from begin a rigid, shriveled creature, I can opt to love and live this moment—this enigmatic, profound moment that exists in this Land of Mystery—a moment being produced for me by this Profound Reality. And to do this I need to trust the trustworthiness of Profound Reality. And in order to trust the trustworthiness of Profound Reality, I will need to have the trustworthiness of Reality revealed to me—perhaps in the Exodus event—perhaps in the Christ event—perhaps in the Buddha event—perhaps in the teachings of Lao Tzu—perhaps in the teachings of Mohammed. All these religious movements and others may provide us their gifts in regard to this proficiency for blissful realism. Much more will be explored on this topic in Parts Two and Three.

PART TWO

Knowing Profound Reality with Religious Metaphors Approximately

Part Two is about religion as a social practice that can make more likely the gift of an experience of Profound Reality, the overwhelming essence of which has already been sketched in the Introduction and Part One. In this Second Part we will explore further the essence of Profound Reality and how our long-standing religions practices have and can continue to assist us to discover and take in our Profound Reality experiences.

In Part Two I will explore three main topics:

A. What is Religion?
B. The Wisdom of Primal Metaphors
C. Some Conclusions about Primal Metaphors

A. WHAT IS RELIGION?

When all religion is humanly created

WE DO NOT KNOW AN answer to this question, when we only know the names of many religions and have perhaps practiced aspects of several of them. But if this question means "what is good religion?" as distinguished from the many perversions of each type of religion, then this question becomes much more testy. And when the question is about having a general definition of religion that applies to all religions as an important social process that appears in almost every human culture, we enter into a key discussion about human life on planet Earth.

Nevertheless, let us start with the notion touched upon in Part One of this book, that there is such a human experience of our awareness of our *profound consciousness of Profound Reality*. This enigmatic "Profound Reality" or "Land of Mystery" is a metaphor with which to communicate our experience of this "Finality of Reality" toward which all our approximate knowledge is approximating.

This Profound Reality is a realism inaccessible to our finite mind's ability for storing rational contents. Nevertheless, we find that our expression to one another of anything about this direct experience of a profound consciousness of Profound Reality requires for our human sharing something different than the knowledge of natural science, or the insights of contemplative inquiry, or the savvy the interpersonal wisdom, or the know-how of sociological workability. Profound consciousness of Profound Reality is shared with metaphorical expressions—parables, koans, rituals, icons, myths, poetry, song, dance, etc.

We require such cryptic devises of a human mind's creation in order to share our profound human consciousness of the Profound Reality that is beyond our rational reach. However paradoxical this may sound, we can, amazingly enough, describe something of the essence of our experiences of Profound Reality.

By "consciousness" I mean the *awareness* and the *freedom* of the ordinary natural consciousness with which members of the human species are using for communication through art, language, and mathematics as well as through the types of intelligence we share with the other species. By "profound consciousness" I mean this same plain ordinary human consciousness when it is being conscious of Profound Reality. Then we can also notice that our consciousness and our profound consciousness are aspects of our biological life that accesses this Profound Reality of which natural human consciousness can be aware.

"Religion" then, is any set of practices (group and/or solitary) being done by human beings with some metaphorical creations from this or that aspect of human cultural life—which comprise a set of practices has the purpose of awakening human consciousness to our living "touch" with Profound Reality. Here is a story that may help us to focus our fragile minds on this phenomena:

> *A student of Buddhism asked his teacher if meditation caused enlightenment. "No," said the teacher, "enlightenment is an accident. Meditation only makes you more accident prone."*

This insight can be expanded to all religious practices. No religious practice causes the awakenment to profound consciousness of Profound

Reality. Profound consciousness is the essence of who we essentially are in our awakenment to a profound consciousness of Profound Reality. And it is Profound Reality that is rescuing us from our estrangements from Profound Reality. We humans are all sharing in the substitute "realities" we mistake for Reality.. This healing event is variously called "illumination," "grace," "salvation,""justification," "sanctification," "enlightenment" or something else. A religious practice can only make us more prone to having such "healing events" happen to us. The happening is not caused by us, the happening happens to us or it doesn't happen to us. We never accurately experience ourselves as in control of this happening. And our religious practices, whatever they are only make this happening more likely.

If this healing does happen to us, what we are being healed from is our own deep sickness and our culture's deep sicknesses—a sickness that amounts to attempting to rebel or escape from the ever-present Profound Realty from which there can be no actual escape and with regard to which no rebellion can win. This is how are escapes are a sickness: they undo our optimal aliveness.

One popular attempted escape today is the assertion that there is no Profound Reality—that realism is left to each of us to create and cling to—that realism is whatever view of reality we like better than the Profound Reality that is actually confronting us, and that is auditing us—and that is revealing to us the ways that we have gone astray from Profound Reality..

Such an awakening to Profound Reality includes the motivation and the "how" of living our whole lives from our awareness of Profound Reality. A religious practice may include being a sub-culture of some group of people, but that is not the essence of being a religion. A good religion is a practice that seeks to make this profound consciousness of Profound Reality more likely. We may identify with being a certain religions practice, but profound consciousness is not an identity along with athlete, singer, citizen, the religion we practice, or the profession/ work that we pursue. Profound consciousness is the gift of being encountered by Profound Reality and rather than fleeing or rebelling, accepting our acceptance by Profound Reality into a total forgiveness and a fresh start in realism. Our valid religious practices encourage such healing happenings and the creative living out of those happenings as the meaning and essence of our lives.

Here is a poem that expresses somewhat the discussion above:

I am an alert deer.
Dread gets my attention
and I can move quickly
in many directions.
I am a surprise
and hard to predict.

A fear of real enemies
is the alertness of a deer,
While my alertness is
dread of a mysteriousness
no deer can know.

And I am unpredictable
in a manner
no deer can match.

Dread of the Unfathomable
is my essence.

Surprise
is my being.

B. THE WISDOM OF PRIMAL METAPHORS

BY "INTER-RELIGIOUS ERA" I MEAN that every large city is populated with at least small numbers of people practicing most of the long-standing religious practices of the planet. Even my small northeast Texas town of Bonham has had for over a decade until that gym closed a Tai Chi class meeting twice a week attended mostly by conservative Christian practitioners. The very language of the Tai Chi teachings have their origins in oriental religious antiquity.

I am going to describe briefly six different ways that religions practices in six different Earth areas began in their deep antiquity, creating religious practices. The first area I will examine is the often called "Arabia"—the area that was home to the origins of Judaism, Christianity, and Islam. The descendants of Arabian antiquity created religious practices that found ways of adapting to the quite different antiquity of Greece culture. These two primal metaphors of antiquity are present in modern Judaism, Christianity, and Islam. Much recent effort has gone into exploring this dialogue often called "Athens and Jerusalem." I will pull these two antiquities apart, beginning with the Primal Metaphor of Arabia.

1. The *"Abrahamic-Dialogue"* Metaphor

As a first example of a primal metaphor of religious practices I am going to show how a basic metaphor of religious reflection is present in the very ancient Biblical stories of Abraham and Sarah. These mythic dialogues are about I-Thou relations with Profound Reality, personalized as dialogue with the all-powerful Yahweh. These old stories have been foundational for Judaism, Christianity, and Islam—three of the major religions that originated in the sector of the planet that is often called "Arabia"—North Africa, Saudi Arabia, Israel, Palestine, Jordan, Iraq, and a few more places)

The myths of Abraham feed off of an actual historical journey of a culture of people in the years following 1800 BCE—people who migrating from the highly civilized city called Ur on a river valley of what is now called "Iraq"—a migration to the coastal area of the Mediterranean that we now call "Palestine" or "Israel." Later, many members of this culture of people were slaves in Egypt and some of them fled into the wilderness of Jordan and Sadia Arabia. around perhaps 1300 BCE with that amazing personage called "Moses."

The myths of Abraham and Sarah that we have in our Bibles begin to be written up as lasting tradition around 1000 BCE. In these now familiar biblical stories, Abraham is pictured as a son of parents who were living in Ur. The qualities of these Abraham and Sarah myths embody a "primal religious metaphor" that characterized that region of the planet long before the Abraham myths were composed and remembered. These strange stories of Abraham and Sarah reflect a particular "primal religious metaphor" and these stories can assist us to see what a "primal religious metaphor" is.

The "Abrahamic-Dialogue" metaphor was made from ordinary, temporal, mental content found in the interpersonal approach to approximate truth—that is, this particular primal religious metaphor makes use of mental content from an I-to-I type of conversation—a person-to-person type of mythic devise. The Jewish theologian, Martin Buber, spoke of this as the I-Thou relation and applied his careful thinking to both the persons-to-person relation and to the person-to-Profound Reality relation.[6] This I-Thou mythic expression is found throughout the Hebrew and Christian scriptures in which we see, first of all, the myths of Abraham's human conversations with Yahweh—a personification of Profound Reality.

So let us notice the presence of this I-Thou metaphor in the stories of Abraham. First of all, we hear the story about Abram and Sarai leaving the city of Ur, not knowing where they were going. Abram, as he was then called, was convinced from his dialogues with Profound Reality that he was being promised the blessing of being the father of millions if he left his home city, his parents, his whole way of life and began anew in an unknown land. Then after settling in this "promised land," we hear a story of an explicitly spelled out dialogue in which Abraham is pursuing some outright bargaining with Profound Reality over how many righteous humans in the horrifically wicked cities of Sodom and Gomorrah it would take to save these cities from their coming destruction. Abraham is concerned for the lives of his nephew Lot and his family. Abraham's extended dialogue with Yahweh is printed out in the scripture. The end of that story was that Lot and his family had to leave these doomed cities. Our requests of Profound Reality do not always have the same answer we ask for.

Other I-Thou dialogues with Profound Reality took place in two other significant Abrahamic stories. Abram and Sarai, now past the age of child bearing, still have no child though which the promise of descendants can be carried out. Then three messengers from Profound

---

[6] Buber, Martin, *I and Thou*

Reality come by their tent and announce that Sarai was to bear a child. Sarai laughed and Abram, now Abraham, apparently just stared in wonder. Sarai, now Sarah, did indeed, according to this story, bear a child. This story exaggerates how Isaac is a miracle child given by Profound Reality, but, if we think about it, being a miracle child is true of all children. Yet though all children are the gift of Profound Reality, this child Isaac is being viewed by Abraham as fulfilling the promise made to him by Profound Reality that he was to be the father of descendants as numerous as the grains of sand on the sea shore.

Notice that the underlying religious metaphor, in operation in these stories, is "dialogue with Profound Reality." What we have going on here is a vision that the essence of being a human being is "dialogue with Profound Reality." Profound Reality speaks and we humans respond by speaking back about which Profound Reality speaks again. Profound Reality has the first and last word, but humans also have a say in their destiny. This is all myth or metaphor, but the meaning of this primal metaphor explores the nature of human life in its deepest aspects.

The last Abraham story that I am going to cite as an illustration of Abraham's I-Thou relation with Profound Reality that has had whole books written about it. Both theologians and philosophers have argued about this topic until the present day.[7] Like the above examples, this preposterous story is a myth, shaped as a tale about an I-Thou-relation with Yahweh.

In this story, Abraham in his ongoing conversations with Profound Reality becomes aware that all the gifts from Profound Reality have to be given back to Profound Reality, including the gift of Isaac that is so central to Abraham's whole life. Abraham sees this awareness of giving back as his own command to be the very knife that gives Isaac back. So he proceeds to do so.

---

[7] Søren Kierkegaard wrote a whole book abut this story: *Fear and. Trembling.*

This story seems outlandish, but let us notice that it is true that all parents have to give back their children to Profound Reality—if not with the death of their children, then when in their children's life times, their children move away to live their own lives rather then continue to live in dependence on parents. This does entail a type of giving-up children faced by all parents. Abraham grasps somehow that not clinging to Isaac is part of his Profound-Reality dialogue. In the completion of this strange story, Profound Reality appears to say to Abraham, "OK you have done the command of giving back Isaac, I am providing for you a goat in yonder bush for your symbol of this needed sacrifice. Abraham grasps this as Profound Reality doing a re-giving of Isaac to be his hope of continuing the promise of Profound Reality for Abram to become Abraham, father of numerous descendants.

As we look back on this story in the context of this I-Thou dialogue with Profound Reality, we see that this *giving back* is the seed that Abraham is passing along to so many people. Abraham's descendants are those who live out "*the spirit seed of giving back all their gifts to the Giver.*" Other Genesis and Exodus stories continue this narrative of such "giving back"—especially Jacob, Joseph, Moses, and an ongoing mighty chorus of Jewish, Christian and Islamic religious prophets and practitioners who see Abraham as their spirit father.

Within these wild myths we can see the outlines of a primal religious metaphor that is very ancient and that is foundational for these three Arabian-origin religious heritages. Though massively influential, this primal metaphor "the Abrahamic-dialogue with Profound Reality" has been difficult for twenty-first century people to embrace. Partly, this has been due to mistaking the "Thou," naming of this "Profound Reality" dialogue partner, as a literal Personage in a literal other-world or spirit realm I can go to after my death. Even if we try to believe this, we know, secretly perhaps, that this is spooky talk—even oppressive talk when we think of this so-called heaven as a reward for being "holy." So, perhaps many of us have simply dismissed all three of these widely practiced religions as superstition.

There is a middle way between these dogmatic and anti-religious extremes. We can view this primal religious metaphor as simply a metaphor constructed from part of our approximate knowledge—our temporal I-Thou interpersonal life with other human beings, and with other animals. This dialogue experience is used here as metaphorical talk about a Real "Encounter" that is meeting us in every "that" of our lives. This "Eternal That' is not a Big Person, but a very big Mystery that we have no concept with which to contain it or control It—a Mystery and a Power that does not go away. Nevertheless, we can share with one another, as humans have done for thousands of years, our experience of this Final Mystery and use this I-Thou metaphor to talk about our experiences with the Profound.

This very ancient religious metaphor can come alive for us and unite us with millions of great souls who have used this metaphor metaphorically even though they did not have our contemporary sort of language to speak about metaphors. Seeing that there are other primal metaphors than the I-Thou metaphor is an attitude of mind that is happening today among the best theologizing going on in Jewish, Christian, and Islamic communities of contemporary reflection.

There are at least five other primal religious metaphors than the one I just introduced. Here is how I am naming these other metaphors: (2) the "That-Thou-Art" metaphor of ancient India, (3) the "Yin/Yang" metaphor of ancient China, (4) the "Designing-the-Unstoppable-Flow" metaphor forged in the ancient Americas, (5) the first of all primal religious metaphors that arose in primitive Africa that I am calling the "Heart-Beat" metaphor, and (6) the "Ordering-the-Absolute-Wonder" metaphor of northeast Mediterranean Europe—a religious heritage we associate with Athens Greece rather than with Jerusalem, the home of the Hebrew heritage featuring the metaphor of Abrahamic dialogue. All three of these major religions of Arabic origin (Judaism, Christianity, and Islam) have now been entangled with the Athens-elaborated primal metaphor.

Each of these two metaphors is a temporal human creation (not itself Eternal), but it has been used to access, share, and live our human lives in awareness of that Eternal Profound Reality that is too much for any mere human set of words or thoughts. Only consciousness, acting as consciousness can access connection with Profound Reality. I will show how we can notice the presence of five more of these primal metaphors that have been and still are useful to more fully share our awarenesses of and our connections with Profound Reality.

2. The "*That-Thou-Art*" Metaphor

A very different primal religious metaphor is foundational in the religious antiquity of the continent we once called "India." Today, that modern continent is broken into India, Pakistan, and Bangladesh. These three locations are now formed by many forces other than this very ancient Dravidian metaphor I and going to explore—the British rule (1852-1947 CE), the Muslim invasions (beginning in the eleventh century CE, Also, long before these Muslim invasion of India, the Indo-Aryan invasions in 1500-1200 BCE swamped this complex land. In these earliest religious ferments, we find the origins of Hinduism, Buddhism, and several other long-practiced religions.

This primal religious metaphor that I will attempt to describe was given sophisticated expositions in the Upanishads of Hinduism that were written in Sanskrit in the centuries following 800 BCE until perhaps 500 BCE. This is the same time period in which the prophets of Israel and Judea were giving a similar sophistication to the Abrahamic metaphor described above. The antiquity of the India-originated metaphor is vividly present in Hinduism and in the early India Buddhism. The origin of this metaphor reaches back before the Indo-Aryan invasions to an India impacted by a highly developed Dravidian civilization that originated along the Indus river beginning 2600-1900 BCE. The notion of hierarchical civilization had migrated from the Nile Valley civilizations of Egypt through Black Africa and then by sea to what is now part of Pakistan. The Dravidians gave their version of civilization a different flavor than its Arabian and African versions. This primal religious metaphor was giving cultural shape to that civilization development.

We can most easily get a glimpse of the essence of this ancient metaphor from the Upanishad summarization of it in this bit of simple poetry "That Thou Art." "That" in this cryptogram means the ever-present externally experienced Final Mysterious of Profound Reality that the Hindus called "Brahman." "Thou" in this "That-Thou-Art"cryptogram is about the companion mystery of the ever-present "Great Self" or "Atman" in Hindu lore. "Brahman" and "Atman" are One Profound Mysterious Reality (That I Am). Both. Brahman and Atman are present in the same moment of real experience. The more outward-facing Brahman experience and the more subjective-facing Atman experience happen together. For those who get the truth of this teaching, the essential "I" is exalted and the essential "That" is humanized. This is an ancient India way of metaphorically speaking of this profound consciousness (Atman) being aware of Profound Reality (Brahman).

The temporal content used for this primal metaphor is taken from the contemplative approach to truth, rather than from the interpersonal approach to truth emphasized in the Abrahamic dialogue metaphor of

Arabia. The interpersonal approach to truth is also present in the culture of India, but the India primal metaphor found in the Upanishads and pervading so much of the religious reflections of India depends almost entirely on the contemplative approach to truth, rather than the interpersonal approach to truth.

Hindu religious practice does feature dialogue with many gods, but in the deepest Hindu thoughtfulness, all these gods are "transcended" in the Brahman/Atman state of consciousness. The gods are thereby demoted to semi-lasting temporal aspects of human life: they are at most sub-parts of the profound subjective experience of the Brahman/Atman unity. Thus the India address to our Western religious conversation is not about polytheism, as understood in the lessons of Arabic heritage. The radical monism of India is also different from the radical monotheism of Arabia, even though it is the same Profound Reality being referenced.

I want us to notice the fact that these two different regions of the planet show us how the same Profound Reality can be explored very differently. Nevertheless, the Brahman "THAT" and the Almighty "Yahweh" reference the same Profound Otherness and the Atman "I" and the "Holy Spirit" reference the same deep un-self (beyond ego Atman) I am calling "profound consciousness." This profound consciousness is a level of freedom as well as a level of awareness. And with these levels of awareness and freedom attends a level of love/compassion/buddha-kindness toward our neighbors.

The Buddhism of ancient India sought to clarify that the Atman (Great Self) was not the "ego self" or the "self image" of human construction. In other words, this Great Self was "no self" at all in the most usual senses of the word "self." I take this view of "no self" to mean a reference to the contemplative insight that a ghostly or substantial self is not to be found anywhere in our contemplative awareness of the inner life. The so-called "enlightened self" is a pure freedom that has no resting place in the temporal flow of sensations, emotions, thoughts, and actions. Only as a transcending of ordinary consciousness is the so-called "Atman" one with the so-called "Brahman." These reflections of India Buddhism continue to be used to clarify the India primal metaphor that underlies much Hinduism, Buddhism and other sub-Asian religions.

3. The "*Yin/Yang*" Metaphor

China, Japan, Tibet, Korea, and a number of other Asian cultures created deeply transformed styles of Buddhism after Buddhism combined in China with Taoist and Confucian religious breakthroughs. In the antiquity of these North-Asian cultures we can note a third primal religious metaphor whose temporal imagery in taken from the social-commonality quest for truth, rather than from the interpersonal or the contemplative quests for truth. All four quests for truth go on in every culture, but in the design of a culture's primal religious metaphor, the content is mostly drawn from one of those four types of approximate truth. I will illustrate what I mean by the communal or sociological nature of the Chinese primal religious metaphor with the following spin on the yin/yang symbol found in Taoism.

Pictured here is a complementary twosome that completes a whole. For example white and black are complementary colors on this printed page. With only one or the other color, there would be neither aspect of this picture. A most obvious social example of this "complementary polarity" is North Asia's use of this metaphor to illuminate the relation between nature and human society. For example, let human society be the "yang" (white) or *putting-forth* in union with the *taking-in* of nature's "yin" (black). This means that our human consciousness takes in nature and puts forth society. If human society is the light colored fish in this circle of wholeness, we also see a dark dot of nature in the light fish of society. This means that society is in its essence a natural thing to happen. The light dot in the dark fish of nature can indicates that nature is always being perceived from the point of view of society.

Society and nature are not entirely separate processes. Nature and society form a polarity that is fundamentally complementary, rather than conflictual. There is no human society separate from nature. And there is no natural Earth to which we human relate except the Earth as viewed from the imaginations of a human society. For example, humans once saw the Earth as a flat pancake, astronomers calculated otherwise, and we now have photographs of this blue, white, and brown ball from the perspective of the moon. Whatever be our scientific view of the Earth, we can still view Earth as yin and the human as yang in a complementary polarity of mutually enriching realities.

We have one environment composed of a natural environment and a social environment. These two environments do not have to be at war. We can imagine a society that lives within nature without destroying nature. And we can imagine a nature that can viewed as a support for society, rather than being a force against which society must fight. The tension that is real between nature and society can be seen as complimentary, rather than conflictual. Such vision is part of the implications of the Yin/Yang primal metaphor for profound understanding.

This yin/yang type of relatedness also applies to the awareness-&-freedom polarity within a "whole" that we can call "consciousness." It is awareness that makes freedom possible. It is freedom that gives awareness expression. There is no standing aside from Reality as a mere aware observer. Consciousness is also response-ability or freedom. And our freedom (or response-ability) is simply part of that profound consciousness we approximately take in with a Profound Reality encounter. "*Attentionality*" (or paying attention) means *taking in reality into* our consciousness. "*Intentionality*" (or freedom) means *putting-forth* conscious actions that are "*reality bending.*" Both *taking-in* and *putting-forth* are polar aspects of consciousness that describe what we can mean by the very word "consciousness." Herein is another aspect of the genius of the Yin/Yang primal metaphor.

Both the awareness and the freedom aspects of consciousness are *real* and *good* in the context that consciousness as a whole is real and good. The whole of *human consciousness* has within it this complementary polarity: *attentionality* (yin) and *intentionality* (yang).

We also have experiences in which we face good-and-bad as a conflictual polarity—the options of every either-or choice. "Good" choices as they appears in the yin-yang vision of Reality, means accepting the both-and quality of complementary polarities—such as *nature and society* in the whole of humanly perceived environment, or *attention and intention* in the whole of consciousness. Similarly *Male and female* form a complimentary whole we might name our "biological animality".

"Bad," in the yin-yang vision, can be illustrated with the making of society good at the expense of nature being viewed as bad; or by the making of nature good at the expense of society being viewed as bad. In the yin-yang vision, nature and society form a whole in which both are related to as "good Earth processes or environments." So viewed, our ecological thinking does not have to affirm nature at the expense of society or affirm society at the expense of nature. The yin/yang vision supports finding a form of society and a handling of nature that affirms both society and nature as necessary for the optimization of planet Earth processes.

Today, we very much need ways to affirm our various "wholes," rather than insisting on warfare between these many necessary complementary parts of a whole reality. For example, maleness and femaleness can form a whole, rather than one being bad and other good. We need not replace patriarchy with matriarchy. That would only be revenge. We can find a middle way recommended by a yin/yang vision of our biological gendering. We can be enabled to see that each man has a feminine component and that each women has a masculine component as part of seeing the feminine/masculine complementary tension.

The yin/yang metaphor also questions our miss-use of some of our conflictual pairs in thought: "top-and-bottom," "less-and-more," "better-and-worse." Complementary understandings may apply to many sets of values currently miss-viewed as conflictual. Also yin/yang understandings can give meaning to the whole of realities we describe as two inclusive parts. Such parts do not have to be at war with each other, even though serious tensions may exist between them. Nor do complementary polarities have to be seen as melded into a sameness. Tensions are not ignored. Needless conflicts are avoided. In may be of interest to note that the Chinese revolutionary Mao observed, "Primal contradictions for action can be seen to guide our action."

This yin/yang way of communal reflection can be extended to our experiences of the Whole or Oneness of Profound Reality. In the ancient religious ferment in China we call "Taoism" there were many religious poets besides Lao Tzu. Here is part of a poem by Chaung Tzu, as translated by Thomas Merton. These verses illustrate how this mode of religious expression was used by these early cultures to express what I am calling "the profound human consciousness of Profound Reality." For example, the following poem refers to the Eternal Tao (the Lasting Way)—the Whole that contains all the polarities..

> Tao is beyond words
> And beyond things.
> It is not expressed
> Either in word or in silence.
> Where there is no longer word or silence
> Tao is apprehended.[8]

Implied in this and other such cryptic poems, the "Eternal Tao" is revealed to be a mode of devotion to Profound Reality. Taoist thinking is a type of dualism in which a yin-yang pair of factors implies a *whole* of which this particular yin and yang are two complementary parts. Such a quest for truth is actually an emphasis upon *wholes*, more than *parts*. The "Eternal Tao" is what we have when the most inclusive dual parts reveal one Final Whole. I am using here the capitalized word "Whole" to correspond with the Oneness of Profound Reality being indicated in the radical monotheism of the West. A devotion to Profound Realty is also being implied in the above poetry, for the Taoist practice assumes a love of realism that extends to a love or devotion to that "Eternal Way" of Profound Reality Wholeness. The Eternal Tao is the Way it Is. In these poems, it is implied that the Eternal Way is the "authentic Way" for humans to take.

---

[8] Merton, Thomas, *The Way of Chaung Tzu*. 152

4. The *"Designing the Unstoppable Flow"* Metaphor

When the Europeans arrived in the Americas, the Aztec civilization was an empire that covered at its greatest extent most of northern Mesoamerica. This empire was centered in what is now Mexico City and had ruled the large space since 1345 CE until it was conquered by the Spanish in 1521 CE. Another strong civilization, the Incas, then ruled a large portion of South America, in the Andean Mountains of what is now Columbia and Ecuador on the north and south to parts of Bolivia, Peru, and Chili. The Incas had existed as an expansive empire since 1438 CE until its Spanish conquest in 1533. Sill older strong civilizations had existed in the Americans. Since about 1600 BCE, the Olmec civilization had lived along the Gulf Coast of Mexico until around 350 BCE.

These facts are surprising when we note that the civilization type of society did not reach England until shortly after 800 BCE when the Romans came to that island. The earlier societies in England, such as those that built Stonehenge and other large-stone structures, were foraging and agricultural-village associations, not yet city-centered and hierarchical civilizations.

In general human history, the first city-centered hierarchical "civilization" may have appeared in the city state of Uruk in what is now Iraq, as early as 4500 BCE. This idea of "a hierarchical ordered civilization" spread to Egypt by 3200 BCE and from the Nile civilization spread south into black Africa and then by sea to the India/Pakistan area by 2500 BCE and still later to China. So we are given to wonder how the idea of civilization arrived to the Americas by 1600 BCE. Was it boats of some kind or was it walking across the Aleutian straits from northeast Asia? Were these American cultures an independent development from northeast Asian sources? The Americas are full of mysteries. And for the most part, the humans that lived here were separated from the rest of the human population for at least 15,000 years.

The complex migration history to the Americas, brought a unique variety of hunter-gatherer tribes, early agricultural village associations, as well as hierarchical civilizations. All of these very different forms of society appear to have some cultural affinity with one another. Also, this entire group of societies have affinities with northeastern Asia. But most of the migrations from Asia took place 30,000 to 10,000 BCE, making the primal metaphor of these American continents significantly different than what we see in 800 BCE Asia.

I am going to use the Aztec civilization, about which we know a great deal, to provide some clues to the essence of the primal religious metaphor that developed in the ancient Americans. The famous Aztec calendar of events that made up the religious/secular cycle of the year for that civilization provides a good place to begin describing this primal religious metaphor that developed in the Americas. The schedule of activities on that calendar contained a polarity of times for maintaining an ordered society and other times for celebration ("fiesta the Spanish called it, and "pow-wow" is a term used by the English in the north). In the Aztec version these periods of celebration on the calendar were rather wild celebrations that abandoned many of the social norms and seemed to taste a type of chaos in relation to those social norms that pertained to the more survival-ordered periods of the calendar.

Getting back to understanding the primal religious metaphor of the Americas, these chaotic fiesta celebrations have a bit of similarity with the Sabbath tradition of Judaism and Christianity—1 2 3 4 5 6 Sabbath is somewhat like the Aztec survival-oriented work period and then Fiesta. Perhaps humans need this sort of rhythm to our social flow of customary time designing. The difference between the fiesta of the Americas and the Arabian Sabbath is that the fiesta break in the social time flow is like entering into a whole new society. Fiesta almost completely breaks the flow of the practical work society geared to get social survival accomplished. Fiesta is like returning to the chaos from which regular society is built by humans from the chaos of possibilities in the continual art of building society. After fiesta, the work society is rebuilt, probably quite like the work society that was left, but not necessarily so. Certainly, a high consciousness about society building was keep in mind.

The Native American tradition of the sand painting give us another feel of this sort of temporal religious creativity. An elaborate design with sands of various colors is made. Then the entire sand art-piece is brushed back into chaos. This gives us a spirit level feel about social life not found so vividly on the rest of the planet.

Yet these fiesta celebrations take place within the one calendar of social life. The polarity of these two types of calendared periods seems to portray a similarity with the yin/yang complementary pairing of nature and society. going on in China and north east Asia.

Another example of such complementary pairing can be seen in the myths and icons of Quetzalcóatl, (from quetzalli, the green tail feather of the quetzal bird and coatl, "snake"). This "Feathered Serpent" was one of the major deities of the ancient Mayan and Aztec pantheons of religious icons. The bird aspect is a symbol for flights into the deepest states of wild consciousness, while the snake celebrates our crawl in common earthiness. We may have in this symbol a reference to an ancient form of religious metaphor that was developed in a different way than described with the yin/yang poems and practices of Chinese Taoism.

Because this primal religious metaphor development of the Americas separated so long before the 700 BCE Asian Taoism developments., we are herein inquiring into a human cultural development that commenced its separation from Asia as early as 30,000 BCE. Therefore, there was certainly time for the possibility of a separate primal religious metaphor development within the Americas from the primal religious metaphor that was being developed in North Asian Taoism in 700 BCE.

A preoccupation with human communal life and with a balanced relationship between nature and society are two ways these two vast regions of religious culture are somewhat similar. However important these similarities may be, it is certainly true that the religious developments of the Americas merit their own open-ended religious research. We certainly have much to learn from a branch of humanity that separated from the rest of us so early.

In addition to our understandings of Mesoamerica religious we also need to read about the Inca civilization and perhaps visit the people and ruins of the highlands of Peru and Bolivia. We also need to hear the voices of North American native cultures and listen for their primordial rumblings. All these different cultures of peoples give us insights into the primordial religious metaphor that can be found to unite the pre-European invasions and to provide their different lessons for all of us about our humanity and the depths thereof.

My brief spin on the Native American primal metaphor is another example of "approximate knowledge." Even though I have read books, visited peoples, places, museums, and ruins across the Americas, attended drumming, dancing, and sweat lodges conducted by Native Americans, as well a attended workshops taught by Native American teachers, I am still a beginner in my awareness of the unique qualities of these peoples.

Indeed, if any native American wishes to take offense that I have claimed to know anything about their primal religious metaphor, I welcome the insight. I want only to claim that I see a primal religious metaphor characterizing these many peoples in their religious and social practices. I also wish to challenge in myself any supposed "truth" of an "absolute" sort we can find in Euro-American persons claiming a sort of arrogant and controlling knowledge, so popular among we children of Athens and Jerusalem culturing.

5. The *"Heart-Beat"* Metaphor

According to a large number of scholars, Sub-Saharan Africa, Black Africa, gave birth to our homosapien species. It is frequently argued that we humans are all "out of Africa." So let us suppose that the primal metaphor for this African region was surely the very earliest primal metaphor in this typology. Some contemporary scholars of African cultures have described the religious roots (the primal metaphor) of early African cultures as based on the heart-beat, the rhythm of our vitalities as a human body. Hear is another name for this primal religious metaphor that I and others have formed from our meager gatherings of African lore: "Attunement with the Final Rhythm."

I believe with some firmness that such a primal metaphor does underlie the native religions of Sub-Saharan African. We students of US slave and ex-slave culture also have a taste of African culture, especially in the music that has been developed from these sources. With a deep emersion in this music we can see, or perhaps feel, a primal metaphor that has to do with the motions of the body and the motions of the inner being of the human. This primal metaphor has to do with drum beats and whole-body dances. It has to do with the primary energies of nature, with the way an antelope moves or a lion moves or a human moves.

This primal metaphor in contrast with the above five is rather stark. If persons creating religion in the style of the primal metaphor of sub-Saharan Africa were to paint saintliness on a specific human with a halo, that halo would best be painted around the entire body, not just the head as we often find in the European West. In these African sensibilities, "saintliness" involves the movement of limbs, the core torso, the head also, the blood, the breath, the sensations, the emotions—all these moving parts. The interactions between these vitalities constitute the "place" of human authenticity. Profound Reality is also viewed as a deep movement or rhythm—a raw underlying vitality. This Profound Rhythm is expressed in drum beats and dances and other arts and religious practices that awaken a human unity with the "Inclusive Vitality" of the cosmos. I have heard it said by one African scholar, I forget whom, that if the French philosopher Descartes could say, "I think, therefore I am," a reflective sub-African shaman might say, "I dance, thereby I be."

Some of the oldest known paintings of humanity appear in those wondrous 30,000 year old caves of wall art found in southern France. In spite of their European location, those paintings reflect the early migrations of humans out of Africa, so very likely these paintings are expressing the ancient primal religious metaphor of sub-Saharan Africa. On the uneven walls of one of these caves are expressively painted animals that seem to move. Two bison fight each other, or perhaps dance with each other. The place is almost alive with motion. These caves were not where people lived. They were places for ritual. They may have been sites for music and dancing. Some archeologists have tested the acoustic qualities of these painted caves and contrasted them with similar caves that are unpainted, and they found the painted ones are acoustically superior. However that may be, these wall and ceiling paintings likely expressed the awe of a place of "worship," using an African primal metaphor of very deep antiquity. Herein we surely have some hints about this more than 30,000-year-old religious culture of Africa. So let us approach all the attention that has been given to the simple vital movements of those paintings as another clue to the primal metaphor of Black Africa.

Slowly, we U.S. citizenry of European descent are coming to appreciate the power of the African culture that came to the American continents on slave ships. Especially the music composed in the southern states is making an enormous impact on all of us. Yet again, I must confess, much more work than what I have suggested is needed for our clarity about the sub-African primal metaphor.

6. The *"Ordering-the-Absolute-Wonder"* Metaphor

This sixth-to-be-described primal metaphor reached some of its earliest sophisticated forms in Persia, Greece, and Rome. I have left it last among these brief descriptions, because most of we Europeans and American immigrants from Europe do not claim to have a primal religious metaphor—at least, no primal metaphor other than the Abrahamic metaphor that was the first to be described in this brief overview.

The brightest religious thinkers among us, however, have compared the antiquity of Athens with the antiquity of Jerusalem as those two quite different roots of primal religious metaphors mingled on European soil—sometime competing, sometimes enriching each other. I am calling the primal religious metaphor that was foundational to the thoughtfulness of Socrates, Plato, and Aristotle as "ordering the absolute wonder." Though that name may make us think of "physics" rather than the "religions" of this area, both the physics and the pre-Hebraic religions of this region witness to an ancient primal metaphor found in ancient Persia and Greece.

I find several prominent physicists, such as Richard Feynman and Brian Swimme, clear that their expanding physics is also expanding an awareness of that everlasting Mystery allied with their expanding approximate knowledge of nature. I don't remember who is was that alerted me to the following strange truth that: "The more we know about nature, the more we know what we don't know." Surely, this statement reflects a religious awareness. And this awareness can also stand as an illustration of what I mean by the ancient primal metaphor of the Greek inspired people. "Ordering the absolute wonder" is a type of paradox, for the absolute wonder is indeed an irrationality that cannot be humanly ordered. Aristotle, I understand, had a great respect for Awe/Wonder and saw it as a spur for our search to find fresh patterns of cause-and-effect order. Aristotle wished to find order with which to counter the chaos of Wonder or Awe.

Illustrations of this "ordering-the-Wonder" primal metaphor I find in the opening chapter of a book by the outstanding philosopher, Mary Jane Rubenstein: *Strange Wonder* with its wonderful subtitle: *The Closure of Metaphysics and the Opening of Awe.* Here is a quote from her book.

> The double movement of wonder takes us out of the world, *only to put us back into the world,* dismantling old possibilities to uncover new ones, exposing as "wind-eggs" all we think we know in order to reveal everything as different—as more itself—than it had been before. Genuine relation and decision, then, do not depend upon closing off wonder into a momentary "spark," but upon keeping it open.[9]

This "momentary spark" view of wonder Rubinstein referred to in an earlier passage in her book with this comment about Aristotle:

---

[9] Rubinstein, Mary Jane, *Strange Wonder: The Closure of Metaphysics and the Opening of Awe,* Columbia University Press: New York, 2011, page 60

"It is Aristotle who first proposed a remedy for wonder in the knowledge of cause and effect. He explained that while philosophy begins in thaumaxein [wonder] 'it must in a sense end in something which is the opposite' . . . Aristotle values wonder because it prompts the learner to find the causes of that which confounds him."[10]

Aristotle's view of the place of wonder persists in some of the scientific philosophizing in our century. Wonder does inspire thoughtfulness to replace wonder with rational order—cause and effect, probability patterns, and other means of giving human understanding to what was previously baffling.

But the deeper insights of Rubinstein and, she claims, of Socrates is that wonder can stay open. She further explains that wonder is both what is stunningly attractive and dreadfully repelling. This is why humans are motivated, in the first instance, to replace wonder with order.

Nevertheless, the whole order of any culture of humans might be pictured as a small boat on a vast ocean of wonder. Let us say that when we are born, we are living at the stern of this cultural boat with little sense that there is something more. As we walk toward full adulthood, we come to the prow of this boat moving into the wonder of a mystery that never goes away. We can then retreat into the body of the boat and forget that dreadful sight, or we can work with the possibility of making friends with this permanent wonder—this opening of a wonder or awe before an Awesomeness that is our one and only Full Reality. I have capitalized the word Reality to indicate that we, in all our sciences, are doing nothing more than approximating a Profoundly Mysterious Reality that is judging the validity of our scientific approximations.

Socrates was born in 470 BCE and Plato and Aristotle both died in

---

[10] Rubinstein, *StrangeWonder,* page 32

93

322 BCE. The primal metaphor that undergirded their philosophizing was thousands of years older than these luminaries. In the 6th century BCE, this metaphor had flared forth in some sophisticated thoughtfulness in Persia (contemporary Iran) in the somewhat famous thoughtfulness of Zoroaster (Zarathustra).

Zoroaster focused his contributions to our awareness in the context of two everlasting principles: "Ahura Mazda" (meaning "Wise Lord") the compassionate, just, creator of the universe. In this sentence "universe" means the presence of order as opposed to an also continuing chaos represented by Angra Mainyu. This is not the radical monotheism indicated in the dialogues with the One God that I illustrated with the dialogues of Abraham. Zoroaster's contributions featured a cosmic dualism that refers to the ongoing battle between Order found within human minds and the Chaos against which this Order must forever struggle.

Nor is Zoroaster's dualism the same as the Taoist complementary dualism; it is a conflictual dualism—an Eternal fight that characterizes the work of humans in their ongoing quest for a truth by which they can devote themselves (ourselves) to finding order as a guide for our useful behaviors. Herein we find a very old clue to the essence of natural science. Zoroastrianism, as a religion is not, however, merely support for the scientific mind, but a statement of human value—a passionate devotion to order over chaos.

The disciples of this sixth primal metaphor have often moved into an oppressive form of this awareness, namely holding that "the rational is the real" or that "the real is rational." Perhaps they view that humans just have not yet discovered the full rational order. These assertions cannot sit at the table of deep truth with the disciples of the other five prima metaphors described above. Each of them in their way finds the Real a Mystery beyond finding or controlling by the human mind. But if disciples of "Ordering-the-Absolute-Wonder" metaphor can embrace the view that all our rational human ordering, even at its best, is only an approximation of the really Real, then the committed holders of these other five mentioned religious impulses can find themselves in a complimentary relation with the disciples of this sixth-mentioned, primal-religious metaphor.

Holders of the Abrahamic primal metaphor of Arabia feature a conversation with One Overall Wholeness that includes both what can be humanly ordered and what is forever chaos to the human mind. In the Arabian primal metaphor that we associate with Abraham, Moses, Isaiah, Jeremiah, Jesus, and Mohammad, the One Eternal Wholeness is met as a sort of Secrete Wholeness seen by some but not all in the events of natural and human history—as an encounter that always includes Wonder. Wonder remains an encounter to which we can respond with both thoughtfulness and with our raw freedom that does not pretend to have all the answers.

In the Hebrew discussion of the "good," good is being realistic in relation with the Oneness of Reality with which we are forced to contend and are being given the response-ability or freedom to respond. Temporal responses (realistic or not) are required by the insistency of the unstoppable flow of time. Human speech and human whole-body action are both included in this "response to Profound Reality." And this "response to the One" can be said to be required in the sense that we must do something, which may include saying something or not saying something, doing something or not doing anything intentionally.

A response to Profound Reality is intended by human consciousness (by awareness and freedom) rather than simply by thought using our mind. Thought is only part of what is included in a response by consciousness to Profound Reality. Thought may indeed precede the whole-body response by consciousness to the Profound Reality we confront. And thought may indeed follow from a Profound Reality confrontation. The Hebrew primal metaphor emphasizes the response of consciousness using the mind to include thinking in the response. This is not the same as following a known set of moralities, customs, norms, patterns, structures, addictions, desires, hopes, etc. All these elements of thought are only considerations for a freedom response, rather than supposing some sort of rational certainty before, during, or after this response.

In the book of Job, a product of late pre-Christian Judaism, the conflictual dualism symbolized in Zoroaster's Persia entered the thought-forms of Abraham's children. We find included in the Job story the poetry of "One God" plus "Satan" as a creature of that One God. "Satan," in this Hebrew context, means a personification of unrealism or illusion that is CREATED BY THE HUMAN SPECIES. Such human creations then become part of the environment presented to us by God in such twisted forms as Rome or Babylon, Persia or Greece, and more recently, England, Germany, and the United States in their fresh form of bigotry, racism, colonialism and more. The Christian theologians Walter Rauschenbusch, H. Richard Niebuhr, and Reinhold Niebuhr all exposed this view of sin as a sociological reality. Marin Luther King Jr was a student of Reinhold Niebuhr. Sin or Satin is a personal as well as a social kingdom of practices in rebellion against the one all powerful Profound Reality, worshipped as God in the Hebraic heritage. "The Kingdom of God" is that part of the sociology of the human species that is responsive to God in free obedience. Christians also call this so-called "Kingdom" the "Body of Christ" or the "Spirit Church."

In Hebraic thought, "Satan" became a power within Yahweh's creation in which freedom has been given to human beings to say no to this All Powerful Yahweh (Profound Reality). Thus the Hebraic view of "Satan" is quite different from the enduring chaos of Zoroaster. In the Hebrew context, "Satan" and "Satan's kingdom" means the human rebellion from a devotion to Profound Reality, Yahweh, the Almighty

One. In the Hebrew story, "Satan" is not about a fight between two more-or-less equal and enduring forces—order and chaos. In the Hebrew and Christian Bibles, "Satan's so-called "kingdom" is present in our lives only by the permission, so to speak, of the One God. Satan's kingdom is a rebellion against the One God—a rebellion that is created by a freedom-possessing humanity given freedom by this One God to honor & obey or to flee & rebel from this One God. The resulting creations of humanity becomes a sociological construction such as Rome as viewed in the cryptic book of Revelation. "Satan" is a creature of God in the sense that God gave humanity the freedom to rebel against this One Profound Reality in all the many forms of unreality made possible by human freedom. In this manner, the classical theologies of Judaism, Christianity, and Islam integrated Zoroaster's conflictual dualism into the radical monotheism of the Arabic primal metaphor.

Nevertheless, Zoroaster's dualism need not be viewed as in absolute conflict with the radial monotheism of Arabia, provided that we view Zoroaster's vision as simply focusing on a different aspect of the truth—namely, that human order and cosmic disorder do in fact conflict—a conflicting that is assumed to this day in the scientific approach to truth. I am proposing the hypothesis that "Ordering-the-Absolute-Wonder" is a primal metaphor useful in both the Persian social reform and in the Greek rethinking of the nature of Truth as an "ordering of Absolute Wonder" The sages of Israel who came up with the book of Job used the metaphor of "Ordering-the-Absolute-Wonder" to enrich another metaphor "The Abrahamic Dialogue with Profound Reality."

And Zoroaster's dualism and the Bible's monotheism do not have to be completely conflictual if the disciples of the Ordering the Absolute Wonder metaphor view this ordering of human truth as always an approximation of the One Profound Reality that can never be fully ordered.

C. SOME CONCLUSIONS ABOUT PRIMAL METAPHORS

1. More Study is Needed on the Primal Metaphors

FIRST OF ALL, THE ABOVE brief descriptions of those six primal metaphors are but sketches—approximations of the full richness of each of these metaphors and its many cultural developments over so many centuries. I might claim a bit of competence on the Abrahamic dialogue metaphor—a metaphor that is so basic to Christian interpretation. I have also worked extensively disentangling the Abrahamic dialogue metaphor from the Ordering the Wonder metaphor. These two primal metaphors have became so entangled within Jewish, Christian, and Islamic theologizing in the West.

More recently, I have also spent considerable time understanding the early Buddhism of India and the early Taoism of China as clues to ancient primal religious metaphors in those two regions. I have also taken note of how Buddhism as it migrated from India to China became a new sort of Buddhism entangling with the Yin/Yang metaphor somewhat as Jerusalem and Athens have entangled their antiquities within Jewish, Christian,,and Islamic theologizing and their complex cultures.

But for the other two primal metaphors sketched above (African and Native America), I only claim enough insight to believe that such primal metaphors do exist. I have not done the research that I would need to do in order to write a competent book on those metaphors. Such books need to be written. I will not be doing that at age 92. I am passing by baton on such tasks along to others. We also need to clarify the relationships among these six efforts of human antiquity to access more fully this Profound Reality we all face.

Whole libraries of books already exist on the unique features of the planet's widely different cultures and religious practices. And many of those books do deal with the deep religious antiquities—revealing something like primal religious metaphors. For example, Bede Griffiths wrote a book published in 1982 entitled *The Marriage of East and West*, in which he contrasted the basic metaphors present in Hinduism and Christianity. Though he did not speak of "primal religious metaphors," he actually explored many aspects of a meaningful conversation between the deep difference between the core religious metaphors of the Sub-Asian and Arabian antiquities. In chapter 4 of my book *The Thinking Christian* I also push along this dialogue between East and West. More books have been and still need to be written on these topics. More attention needs to be paid to the basic insight being suggested here of the existence of these primal religious metaphors that characterize our planet-wide groupings of religious insights and practices.

2. A Primal Religious Metaphor is Usually Taken for Granted

So basic and deep in the life of a culture are these primal religious metaphors that the members of each culture are typically unaware of the primal metaphor or metaphors that are shaping their deepest religious thoughtfulness. A complex mixtures of these very old cultural roots can be extremely confusing and even unreflected upon.

It requires direct encounters with cultures different from our own to even see our own culture clearly. And we are prone not to do open-eyed looking at our cultural roots, for our ego and personality constructions have been built with the gifts of our own culture and therefore our limited views of our own person, that can change with our encounters with cultures that are different from our own. So instead of opening to the gifts of an alien culture, we often persecute those cultures and/or allow ourselves to be persecuted by those cultures.

3. Primal Metaphor Culture Shock

I had the fortunate privilege of living in India for two three-month periods and during each of those times setting up and teaching spirit programs in three-week-long residential training schools. That was an experience of culture shock for me. The mystical or contemplative capabilities of the average thoughtful person in Indian exceeded anything I had experienced in the United States. At the same time the typical India resident had more difficultly with the processes of the more objective thoughtfulness that was easier for most westerners. I had a very different kind of cultural shock when teaching a similar three-week program in Hong Kong in which the Chinese cultural group characterized most of the persons present. Perhaps my most profound cultural shock took place in an eight-week program in Australia in which were present six Aborigines from a pure-blood cultural group from a Presbyterian mission. They knew English and some patterns of the wider world, but they were still embedded in the culture of their own deep past—a past cut off from the Asian continent since at least 25,000 years ago. These were perhaps the strangest people (men and women) I had ever encountered. I was not sure I was always hearing what they were saying or if they were hearing me in what I was saying, Especially the women would answer my questions with stories I did not see how were responses to my questions until later the profoundness of what they had said dawned on me.

4. A Social Creation

Let us be clear that primal religious metaphors are not a feature of nature, but a social creation by human beings developing a culture in which they could survive and thrive. And this means that we do not have one universal primal religious metaphor in which all persons participate in a common way. Also, it has been an easy error for people of each culture to assume that their primal metaphor is in accord with "nature" (that is, with "the essence of being human"), and that the rest of the human beings on this planet are not quite as human as "we." That is not true. Every primal metaphor is only a human creation that abounds in a specific set of human societies. Nevertheless, these various religious traditions can sit a the same table of metaphorical truth and share their stories on the essential matters that are true across these immense barriers of different religious modes of doing basic interpretations of being human with these different primal metaphors.

5. Cultural Relativity

This wonderful term "cultural relativity" is being used for a profound revolution in human awareness and thoughtfulness that has been taking place in recent centuries, as more and more humans are learning to appreciate cultures different from their own. "Cultural relativity" are words that express a strong human cry for all cultures to sit down together at the same tables of inquiry and do some serious exploration of what our deep differences are actually about in their deepest roots and thereby help all of us to understand what each of these long journeys of human living have to contribute to all of us being more human.

Though the above descriptions of primal-religious-metaphor requires much further explorations of each of them, I believe, that this notion of primal metaphors provide a crucial bit of order for cultural-relativity research. We now live in an inter-religious era. For us to continue in our cruel bigotries, arrogant ignorance, needless conflicts, and violent warfare deriving from our religious differences is a clear form of sociological insanity. All of us will need to give up our "absolute certainties" about these rational forms of approximate order. Our authenticity will be taking in this transformation toward viewing our religious and cultural practices, whatever they are, as approximate metaphors rather than as the final or necessary practices for everyone. Also we will need to see the resulting expressions of metaphorically expressed truth that results from these religious practices is not absolute truth. In other words, we need insights into the cultural relativity of our own religious and secular culture, rather than fearing the loss of our supposed absolutes.

Finally, we need the other religions to enlarge the picture within which our own religious practice can be enriched and renewed. This dialogue can best take place within the general mode of truth I am called "approximate knowing." Mysterious Profound Reality and the profound consciousness that is conscious of Profound Reality are ongoing topics of truth built into the whole cosmogenesis of our species. And our cultural, scientific, and metaphorical rationalities about such matters are all approximations at best and often misleading in many of their forms and efforts. Our own culture and its religious practices are never final, for these aspect of our lives are all human inventions that have not dropped down from somewhere nor risen up from anywhere other than human freedom doing its best to survive or perhaps doing its worst to control the uncontrollable.

This "relativity" of every culture, including its religious practices—both the best and the worst of each religion is on the same level of being a finite human creation and its accompanying corruptions. Good and bad religion is similar to good and bad forms of sewage disposal. In fact, good religion is a kind of sewage disposal of bad religion where the sewage in question is illusions, self promotions, and downright lies and cruelty. Religion is a social process with good and bad forms like every other social process. Nevertheless, good religion is an expression of the authenticity of profound consciousness of Profound Reality. Such authenticity is our check on what is good or bad in a religious practice.

6. The Metaphor Mode of Truth

The above summary of six of the primal religious metaphors on planet Earth tell us something about metaphorical expression in general. Our consciousness of our own profound consciousness of Profound Reality cannot be described in the statements of science or any of the other ordinary types of truth quest. The metaphor mode of truth is needed for profound communication, rather than literal science, contemplative confessions, interpersonal case studies, or social history narratives. Elements of these ordinary truth quests can yield imagery that can be used metaphorically to share our experiences of profound consciousness of Profound Reality And even this metaphorical truth expression is approximate knowledge of both Profound Reality and the profound consciousness of Profound Reality. I will illustrate this metaphorical mode of truth by sharing and by commenting upon the parable of the prodigal son—an elaborate metaphor said to be a creation of Jesus himself.

The key for seeing the deep intent of this parable is to understand the father in this story as a metaphor for the Almighty Yahweh, The

Profound Reality. Many modern Christians want to believe that the "father" in this parable is a metaphor for a God less almighty than Yahweh—something more in accord with topics that are more "nice" than the stormy realism of Yahweh. Nevertheless, let us imagine a down-to-earth Jesus who was creating this parable for Jewish persons rooted in over a thousand years of relating to the Almighty Yahweh. Some of us want to forget that Jesus was born a Jew, lived as a Jew, and died a Jew. He never practiced a Christian religion. In his day there was no such thing. Even after the Christ-has-come sermon of Peter at Pentecost and Paul's teaching about the law, the followers of Jesus were still Christ-way Jews. I believe that Christianity as a separate religion was not present in the New Testament writings until the writing of the Gospel of Mark around 65 or 70 CE. And for Mark "God" still means the almighty Yahweh. Mathew is even more Jewish than Mark, and Luke is still speaking to people attending a Jewish synagogue. John is the first the New Testament Gospel writers to assume a Greek audience who is less than familiar with Jewish lore..

In listening to the prodigal son parable, let us set aside any attempts to make some sort of moral or ethical sense out of this old story, typically named "the prodigal son." This parable (Luke 15:12-32), is not about moral advice for sons and fathers, or for employers and their employees, or for slave owners and their slaves, or any thing of that sort. Instead, let is examine how this parable is a metaphor about how we wayward humans might return to Profound Reality from our trips into our grim tragedies of deep despair—that is, from our estrangements from what is Profoundly Real.

Let us view the "father" in this story as an allusion to Profound Reality and to the Jahweh personalization of Almighty Profound Reality. And let us view the two "sons" as allusions to two alternative ways of being related to Profound Reality. Viewed in this way we can see this story as speaking to us about some key religious issues that arises in every century of human life and in every realistic religion on the planet. I am going to quote this parable line-by-line and then comment on the radical nature of these verses.

> *Once there was a man who had two sons. The younger one said to his father, "Father give me my share of the property that will come to me." So he divided up his property between the two of them. Before very long, the younger son collected all his belongings and went off to a foreign land, where he squandered all his wealth in the wildest extravagance. (J. B. Phillips translation)*

To a human father what could be more disappointing than that happening. Not only is this an affront to the father, but it is a pitiful failure on the part of this son's character, good sense, and outright indulgence. As a parable, this story is provoking us about our Profound Reality parentage. The parable refers to going away from our true home in realism into a far land of unreality.

> *And when he had run through all his money, a terrible famine arose in that country, and he began to feel the pinch. Then he went and hired himself out to one of the citizens of that country who sent him into he fields to feed the pigs. He got to the point of longing to stuff himself with the food that the pigs were eating, and not a soul gave him anything.*

This is a strong picture of the state of desperation that can ensue from fleeing Reality. We may have seen how such a state often comes

106

to pass for an extreme drug addict. This story also applies to the state of persons who sell out for wealth and power at the expense of their integrity and common sense. Any flight from Profound Reality places us in a tension with the inescapable forces of Profound Reality. Attempting to win a fight with Profound Reality or to flee from Profound Reality is a hopeless life project. When such a flight continues to its conclusion, we end up in a state of hellish despair penetrating our whole lives.

> *Then he came to his senses and cried out aloud, "Why, dozens of my father's hired men have more food than they can eat, and here I am dying of hunger. I will get up and go back to my father, and I will say to him, "Father, I have done wrong in the sight of Heaven and in your eyes. I don't deserve to be called your son anymore. Please take me on as one of your hired men."*

A shift toward an honest facing of this intense guilt is taking place. So intense is this remorse that being a true son of Reality is too much to even hope for. Just a hired-hand status and some clean grub will do.

> *So he got up and went to his father. But while he was still some distance off, his father saw him, and his heart went out to him. And he ran and fell on his neck and kissed him.*

In this part of Luke's story, Jesus is playing with his listeners at a very deep level. Reality is being pictured as treating our return to Reality with remarkable enthusiasm. In our parable this son does not yet get the thoroughgoing nature of this forgiveness.

> *But the son said, "Father, I have done wrong in the sight of Heaven and in your eyes. I don't deserve to be called*

107

your son anymore . . ." "Hurry!" called out his father to the
servants, "fetch the best clothes and put them on him! Put
a ring on his finger and shoes on his feet, and get that calf
we have fattened and kill it, and we shall have a feast and
a celebration! For this is my son—I thought he was dead,
and he is alive again. I thought I had lost him, and he is
found!" And they began to get the festivities going.

In the telling of this parable, Jesus is pictured as saying something that can seem completely preposterous, if we are viewing this story as being a parable about the essence of Profound Reality in relation to our crazy-making unrealisms. Notice that these sentences are like clubs beading down the last bits of our human moralism. Returning to the mercy of Profound Reality means a fresh start in full sonship, or full daughter-ship, or full innocence, or full saint potential. No period of punishment is required. No apprenticeship is prescribed. Complete restoration is immediately granted by this "Authority" beyond all authority—Profound Reality "herself" (Or Yahweh himself—We can view Yahweh is the Great Goddess in male attire. And Profound Reality actually has no gender except the one we put into our parables. Jesus lived-in a patriarchal era, so all the characters in the above parable are men, even though it applies to women as well.

The prodigal is being given far more than is being asked for by the prodigal human in this story. And if these sentences are not enough to get our attention, Jesus goes on to describe the offense of the elder son to this father's response to his wayward son. Each of us may feel in our own being the feelings of this eldest son who is pictured as faithful to his father. So, as we read the following words, let us keep in mind that in this is a parable in which the "father" is an allusion to Profound

Reality and this elder son is a picture of you and me as the faithful ones to Profound Reality.

> *But the elder son was out in the fields, and as he came near the house, he heard music and dancing. So he called one of the servants across to him and enquired what was the meaning of it all. "Your brother has arrived, and your father has killed the calf we fattened, because he has got him home again safe and sound." was the reply. But he was furious and refused to go inside the house. So his father came outside and called him. Then he burst out, "Look, how many years have I slaved for you and never disobeyed a single order of yours, and yet you have never given me so much as a young goat, so that I could give my friends a dinner. But when that son of yours arrives, who has spent all your money on prostitutes, for him you kill the calf we fattened!" But the father replied, "My dear son, you have been with me all the time and everything I have is yours. But we had to celebrate and show our joy. For this is your brother; I thought he was dead—and he's alive. I thought he was lost—and he is found!"*

The seeming unfairness of this thoroughgoing forgiveness of Profound Reality is rooted in a deep moralism that can be found in almost all of us. We expect Reality to be fair—fair by whatever rules of fairness are embedded in our own psyche. The extravagant mercy of Profound Reality rips to shreds our inherited moralism.

So here is the truth about forgiveness, as revealed in this parable. If the Eternal Profound Reality is not totally welcoming of us back to realism, then no such transformations are possible. We would all be stuck in an ever-descending spiral of guilt. But this is not actually true. Healing happens. The possibilities for redemption from our wrong turns into unreality are real happenings in human life.

Profound Reality, according to this parable, cares nothing for being fair by the standards of any human morality. The focus in this parable is that a truly guilty person can be restored to a fresh start in innocence. Reality is outlandishly happy that a guilty one who is self-condemned to some deadly despair is being restored to aliveness. Herein is the Eternal truth that this parable was created to reveal to individual persons and to communities of persons.

This parable does not support the notion that there is no guilt—that there is no primal human freedom that can go off the track of our Profound-Reality-supported realism. And this parable does not support the notion that everything is determined to work out just as it does, and that no one is to blame for anything. Rather, the revelation about Reality that can be seen in this parable fully acknowledges that guilt is real—that our experience of a valid self-condemnation unto despair is real, and that the experience of despair is a terrible sicknesses.

And this parable also reveals that this terrible sickness can be treated, not by denying our real guilt, but by the divine treatment of total forgiveness for our very real guilt. Forgiveness includes a defeat of unrealism and a fresh start in realism. Forgiveness does not excuse our guilt; rather, forgiveness transforms the meaning of our guilt into done deeds in our own person's past (or in the past of our culture)—a truth about our lives that is now only a case study on how not to live in the future. Our guilt becomes a lesson in realism for our future choices. Forgiveness moves the healing person from the community of becoming ever more unreal to the community of becoming ever more real. Estrangement is a communal as well as an individual sickness. And this sickness is not the same as moral failing. Estrangement is a tragedy to be healed by the "Mercy of the Almighty.

Events of healing forgiveness need not heal everything. The so called "spirit journey" is about the healing of ever deeper layers of our lives. The first step on this journey is trusting the ongoing power of forgiveness by Almighty Reality in its Infinite Profoundness.

Our unreal states of living feed on the basic mistake that our self-constructed ego gets to choose what is real and what is not real. We are called to give that up. Profound Realty alone determines what is real. This Totally Mysterious Truth is the judge of every humanly conceived truth as to whether it is true or not and to what extent it is true. Repentance is a simple **surrender** to what is Eternally so. Paul Tillich tells us that Profound Reality accepts us just as we are: This includes the free gift of **compete forgiveness** and the freedom for a fresh start.

7. The End of the Two-Realm Metaphor

The parable of the prodigal son is a metaphors made from ordinary life and stretched to Eternal import for those who have ears to hear. It is the nature of the Eternal that makes biblical stories cryptic. The prodigal son metaphor assumed a metaphor about Eternity that is now being phased out of use. This now obsolete metaphor is the story about two realms of reality—the ordinary below and the Eternal above. The gods and devils and the King God or Queen Goddess reside in an Eternal realm. All the temporal things that come and go on this time-based Earth comprise the lower realm in this 2-realm metaphor. Some form of this metaphor of an ordinary below and an extraordinary Eternal up above is found in all 6 primal metaphors regions of the planet. We are now experiencing a very radical change in religious sensibilities as we maintain that this two-realm metaphor is now obsolete. It is hard for awakening humans to see that in the past humans used effectively this now obsolete metaphor.

Most important for our current and future grasp of religious history, we must see that the two-realm metaphor was and is a metaphor, not a literal or scientific truth. All those early visionaries who used this metaphor were not literal idiots, they were often familiar with metaphorical thinking even if they did not have the word "metaphor" to distinguish this usage from "scientific."

Also important for our religious clarity today is the vision that a new metaphor is now taking the place of this very ancient two-realm metaphorical story. A one-realm-religious metaphorical story has already dawned. The one-realm metaphor goes something like this: Contents that were formally viewed as activities in an Eternal Space become the Lasting Truth that happens to us as part of each event in the midst of our temporal life happenings. Each healing event frees us to begin some deeper living from the Lasting Profoundness instead of continuing to live only from the temporal and thus passing values. This touch with the Lasting is dependable, and every temporal content is not lastingly dependable. This new metaphor helps us translate for our time all those old-metaphor-stated sayings.

Christians of the second century were called to fight against devotion to a so-called "nicer God" than Jahweh with this creed of their commitment: "I believe in God the Father Almighty, maker of heaven and earth." Today that bit of poetry has become ragged around the words "believe," "Father," and "heaven." Here is poetry that at least indicates some directions for our one-realm expression of Christian faith.

I context my whole life in trust of the GoddessAlmighty, birthmother of all things ordinary and all things extraordinary.

Jesus spoke of the "Kingdom of God" as coming and as already dawning. This was viewed by his listeners as a demotion of the Emperor of Rome to a distant second place to this Almighty King of the mere kings. Similarly, King Herod of Israel, though a low position in the overall "Roman Peace," was, according to the Christmas story in Matthew, threatened with an even lower place by the very birth of Jesus. His infant killing spree was a grim tactic against that demotion threat. Jewish and Christian theologizing use of this notion "King of kings" was not a justification of kingship on earth, but a view that put earthly kings in their place. Today that place is a democracy that holds "kings" accountable—the end of authoritarianism.

A friend of mine ask me some very good questions about the heavenly realm metaphor in the following quote:

> "This brings up a question for me: Who invented the 2-realm (2-story universe) metaphor that has been dominant at least in Western culture for several thousand years? Was this invented by Christianity or was it part of the operating culture and simply used as a framework (metaphor) within which to articulate the church's message?
> What was its gift?" Jim Wiegel

Here are some of my reflections on these questions: The gift of the 2-realm metaphor was in making a distinction between ordinary awareness and profound awareness. Its inadequacy or flaw was not seeing that profound awareness was just an ordinary awareness being made profound by a conscious awareness of the presence of Profound Reality. We do not need to understand our real experiences of these enlightenment moments as a spirit self invading our psyche from a 2nd realm.

Profound Reality is indeed an "other world" in the sense that the natural human intelligence within our ordinary human biology is not capable of comprehending or owning in rational sentences this Profound Reality as some sort of possession. We don't ever "have" this Eternal Truth in a mentally possessed way. Profound Reality is not a set of doctrines or moral teachings. Profound consciousness is not an "owning," but a humiliation of all our owning of knowledge. This humiliation is accomplished by the presence of this Profoundly Unknown Reality—this Absolute Mysteriousness that never goes away into our human smartness.

Who invented this 2-realm metaphor? I am guessing some jet-black African woman poet. When did this occur? Here is my guess: before even one human being migrated out of Africa, this poet woke up to a profoundness she expressed with the 2-realm metaphor. I am guessing that this happened not long after the deep awe-ing of a chimpanzee-like consciousness being enhanced with the gifts of language, art, and mathematics. This *upright-walking-primate-made-human* by the gift of symbol-using intelligence made possible this strange gift of awareness— this "trance" of "other world" sensibility.

I am further guessing that in the centuries following this woman's poem, a more sophisticated level of metaphorical thinking about this 2-realm awareness probably become more expansively "clarified" to more people (with metaphorical rationality languaging) about what had happened to our species. The 2-realm metaphor was a human expression of that added clarity. This metaphor has lasted in a useful way for thousands of years. Today the 2-realm metaphor is dead and is dying for many-to-most people. Our future is to be without it, and there is no going back to it.

Today, we are becoming more clear that there is no factual second story. Even a realm of Final Truth is a fiction. Final Truth is a metaphor for Total Mystery as the Profound Reality experienced by human beings. Even more worrisome for some people is that there is no place to go after we die. We die dead as a condition of our temporal being. "Eternal life" is a quality of unconditioned living that can happen to us now, and this quality of living does live on, just not our awareness of it. And we are now becoming ever more clear about this new metaphorical way of accessing our profound awareness of Profound Reality—The Reality that always Was, is Now, and always will Be.

And we are also becoming ever more clear that Profound Reality awareness can only be expressed with fiction, metaphor, koan, parable, and other cryptic devices that prompt our limited consciousness to be aware of this incomprehensible Profoundness of this Final Reality, of which we humans sometimes have the ability to be aware and to communicate among us with provocative metaphors.

8. The Death of God?

The "Death of God" metaphor can be a misleading way to view the topic of this planet-wide religious shift. What has died is just a religious metaphor—the second realm picture of Gods and Goddesses and devils has simply passed away as a serious metaphor for sharing our deep Profound Reality experiences. Therefore, the Profound Reality that was personified with words like "Yahweh" or "Allah" or "Abba" (papa) has not died. "Yahweh" is a devotional symbol for THAT that does not die. The God of Abraham, Issac, and Jacob has not died. The God of Moses has not died. The God of Deborah, Samual, David, and Elijah has not died.

The German existential philosopher and historian, Karl Jaspers, identified a period in religious history he named "the Axial period." From about 800 to 500 BCE big shifts were occurring all across the then civilized world (This analysis did not include whatever was happening in Sub-Saharan Africa and the Americas.). What Jaspers was noting were events like the dawn of Taoism in China, the Enlightenment of the Buddha and the writing of the Upanishads in India, as well as the proclamations of the Prophets of Israel and Judea, and the teachings of Zoroaster in Persia. What these very different spirit movements had in common was a deepening of human consciousness—seeing that the encountering THAT as more than the cultural canopy and seeing the inward authentic self as more than our cultural conditioning. For example the prophet Jeremiah saw the covenant with Yahweh as more than loyalty to the nation of Judea and the law of Yahweh was something more than a national culture—instead of a book or a culture the law of Yahweh was a covenant written upon the heart that could endure Babylonian captivity. The Axial Prophets of Israel and Judea include at least Amos, Hosea, Isaiah, Jeremiah, Ezekiel, and Second Isaiah.

For all of these prophets Yahweh was an encountering THAT that did not die. Furthermore, this axial awakenment in Judea and elsewhere was not the death of the two-realm metaphor, but an enrichment of its meaning. The death of the two-realm metaphor is also something more than a planet-wide recovery of the Axial awakening. This death of the two-realm metaphor is a consciousness earthquake in planet-wide religious practice that is perhaps greater than all the others. But it is not the Death of God. The Great Goddess, Yahweh, Allah, and the "Abba" (papa) of Jesus is about the Ever-Lasting. Finally, the two-realm metaphor is being replaced by another metaphor for doing our depth religious thinking. I will reflect on that further in the next section.

9. The Other World in the Midst of this World

Perhaps, one of the clearest communication of the new metaphor took place in the work of Joseph Wesley Mathews in his creation of four charts each of which has four treks of different Awe experiences. These four charts were named "The Land of Mystery," "The River of Consciousness," "the Mountain of Care," and "the Sea of Tranquility." Each of these 16 spirit treks is a description of, not a theoretical guess about, 16 existential experiences of the human species of human consciousness being aware of an aspect of THAT Lasting Otherness that is being met by humans in the everyday events of temporal life. These awe-awakening events are something more than what science or contemplative inquiry can illuminate. An Awe experience can, however, be described as consisting of a Great Think of metaphorical power, combined with a Great Feel of emotional overwhelm, consciously taken into human consciousness by a Great Resolve of human freedom.

I will not attempt to further describe these rather complex breakthroughs in this brief book. I have done my most thorough sharing of these four charts of Awe in my book *The Thinking Christian* in which I also describe how the religions of the East have appropriated these four topics differently than the religions of the West (See chapter 4). On the threefold dynamics of Awe itself I have shared much more about this topic in my book *The Call of the Awe (See chapters 1,2,& 3).*

10. Religion is an Inescapable Part of Secular Cultures

Every large city on this planet houses many, if not most, of the major religious practices of this planet. For any nation to call itself a Christian nation or a Muslim nation or a Hindu nation, or a Buddhist nation, or a Jewish nation has become as nonsensical as speaking of a Christian toothbrush or a Christian automobile. A nation state is clearly not a religious organization. A nation is a secular organization as clearly as sewage disposal is a secular institution. "Secular" is not a term of derision; it is simply a distinction: a governmental body of people is a type of covenant, but not fundamentally a covenant to assist human beings in the access of their profound consciousness of Profound Reality. The term "religion" (good religion) can now mean a body of people who are fundamentally in some sort of covenant to assist themselves and other human beings in the access the profound consciousness of Profound Reality. I am strongly suggesting that this definition of religion holds the best of Buddhism as well as the best of Judaism, Christianity and Islam. And these four religions, at their best, define a role for religion in human life also found in Hinduism, Taoism, and many other places as already indicated in the primal religious metaphor discussion. The work of religious practice can be quite tough to do or very easy to do, but in all cases a religious practice is something humans do to make the accident of profound consciousness happenings more likely.

Yet a religious practice is only a prayer for the awakening grace of Profound Reality giving to us the blessings of profound consciousness. Such blessings Reality gives in Reality's own time and in Reality's own manner. Profound Reality is perpetually breaking through the cocoon of our rational approximations of the human-created "reality" that is also often a passionate estrangement from "Reality." Our rational approximations of Reality can also have a smell of holiness, for even an approximation of Reality is in some "measure" "Real." Our estrangements, however, are a willful flight from Reality or a fight with Reality, and these estrangements from Reality have the smell of despair. Despair is the consequence of not being able to escape Reality or win a fight with Reality. And this smell of despair can develop into the severe pain of despair that becomes what we have called "hell."

Thomas Jefferson, James Madison, and others who championed what we have called "the separation of church and state" were early advocates of some now increasingly clear distinctions. This so-called "separation" does not mean that the overall culture of a nation does not impact the religious communities that live there. Nor does this "separation" mean that the mission of each of these religious bodies does not alter the culture, the politics, and the economics of the nation in which each body of religious practice dwells, witnesses, and serves the causes of justice. This relation of state-to-religion and religion-to-state can be a complementary relation in which each one enriches and protects the other. But we Christians or Jews or Muslims or any other religious grouping do not need a governmental body to give preference to "our" religious practice. On the other hand, a government body of realistic politics does profit from what a plurality of religions can provide in pathways to deep realism.

One of those deep realisms has to do with the lack of sovereignty of any king or queen or CEO, or mob boss criminal, of patriarchal head of family. Profound Reality is the One and Only Sovereignty! And that Sovereignty is not an example for or a permission to any human being or any human grouping to be sovereign. The Real Sovereignty is the demotion of every human person and every group of persons from every claim of sovereignty and into roles of ego-freed, creative, servanthood for each other. No government is sovereign. No people are sovereign—no majority, no minority, no one. All human power is limited in the nature of human power by this Profound Reality that is Sovereign—King of kings and Lord of lords.

Also, let us notice that if our witness to our metaphorically expressed religious truth is not powerful enough to make its way without government assistance, the fault is in the quality of our witness, not in a lack of government support. The role of secular government might be appropriately spelled out as protecting each religion from the violence of all the other potentially oppressive religions as well as from all the aspiring dictators, whatever their religion may be. Our human service of the Sovereign Profound Reality implies an ethics that views any constituency-hungry politician who favors one religion as his or her path to power needs to be scornfully satirized and when possible forcefully restrained.

In the Middle Ages of Europe, religious warfare had a place because of the church-state alliances on the part of both forms of Christianity and forms of Islam.. Such a view called forth religious wars for the mastery of state territory by both religion and state. The separation of church and state is a social ethics that is called "democracy." Such an ethics of basic realism does not favor dictatorship of any sort, but rather a democracy of democratic nations across the entire planet.

Today, however, this state-religion ethics ends any need for religious warfare. And no inter-faith peace can be constructed if there does not exist a mutual respect among the disciples of these six primal-religious-metaphor heritages. Religion in each of these six primal origins is experiencing a growing awareness of a common profound consciousness of Profound Reality. Indeed, the descendants of these six primal-religious metaphor creations can become able to sit at the same table of truth and discuss how appropriate statements of truth and justice can be advised for their common culture, politics, and economics of their social places.

Nor do we need to discourage "separate" communities of religion practice. As Jesus is reputed to have said to his disciples, "If other healers are not against us, they are for us." And any "good" religious practice is not itself Profound Reality. A "good" religious practice is only a finite human creation that is assisting humans in an experience by human awareness of the Infinite, Eternal, Lasting Profound Reality to be more likely experienced. There never is a need for one religion in any place to be the only government supported religion. And there never needs to be one religion for any society. The passing of such social arrangements is part of this overall religious shift in the basic religious metaphor of a divine realm along side the temporal realm rather than through the temporal realm..

CONCLUSIONS TO PART TWO

the universality of profound consciousness

The ordinary human consciousness that is present in every human being and elaborated in every human culture is capable of being conscious of Profound Reality, however, in our real world, religion comes into being in human society as an ordinary human practice that aids us in taking a spirit journey away from the momentum of resisting our deep awareness toward letting our authenticity loose. Good religion does not boss, intimidate, or manipulate, but beckons us to see our own estrangements and to find our own path to enlightenment.

The more aware we become of our own profound relations with Profound Reality, the more freedom we have in those relations to live them courageously, creatively, and even blissfully. Profound consciousness is the same profound consciousness no matter what religion or what culture is employed to access that profound awareness and that profound freedom to be actively engaged in making life responses from that profound "basis" of profound awareness and freedom

No truth about this is deeper than the truth that all such profound consciousness is a gift to us, not an achievement, including the freedom which we use to accept the gift of freedom and to live out the results of freedom in real world history. We do not have our freedom as an achievement. We have our freedom and our awareness as an essential factor of our birth in the human species as well as our rebirths into the deep reality possible for our species. As we did nothing to be born, we did nothing to be aware and free. Profound Reality has been and still is taking care of our species and of each one of us through our entire journey through time. What each of us did with our freedom was our own initiated choices among the possibilities offered to us. Nevertheless a total dependence on Profound Reality continues as well as our also being determined by the gift of freedom to make our own continuing response. We have a response ability about what we do with our given freedom.

Such deep truth, when seen and followed, ends religious and cultural bigotries of all types. There is a deep awareness of profoundness that crosses the lines of those very different cultural conditionings and religious practices. I have met this truth teaching sub-Asians in India, North-east Asians in Hong Kong, and Aborigines in Australia. Though these other cultures and religions practices are alien to me and my culture and my religious practices, we are the same humanity,—journeying into the same profound conscious of the same Profound Reality. Following is a story that has grounded for me these almost unbelievable truths:

I was teaching an eight-week residential course in Australia in which six Australian Aborigine adults from an outback Presbyterian mission were in attendance. They had learned English and how to function in twentieth-century Australia, but they still breathed a culture that was more alien to me than I had ever encountered. I was not always sure that I was making contact with these six people.

One morning after I had given a talk on the Land of Mystery, a jet-black slim Aborigine man came forward and said to me, "When you give a talk like that, I can hear you in my own stories." I had no idea what stories he was referring to, but I did get it as I looked into his eyes and saw him looking back at me, that we were made of the same humanity, capable of the same profound consciousness of the same Profound Reality.

My hope for this book is not that it will answer every question we have or that I have said everything I have been given to say in the best possible way, My hope is that these various spins, typologies, and metaphorical poetry, may provoke readers to explore some of the edges of these profound and important matters. Profound consciousness does indeed matter for our human survival and for the optimization of our living in and through these troubled times that are also glorious times if we can see them and live them in a profoundly aware and committed way.

In this inter-religious age, we may be enabled to see visions such as that "the Pure Land" of a type of Buddhism and "the Kingdom of God," understood within the best of Christian theologizing, are both coming, and are also both already here in our actual human history. The calling to our conscious participation in that "Mysterious Land" expressed in these widely differing expressions of our human essence, is requested of us—a singularly unique and yet similar calling for each of us who dare to be authentic humans.

I will end Part Two by sharing one of my poems inspired by the Otherness charts of Joe Mathews that may call to our awareness some of the spirit of bliss that can reach across this wide variety of religious practices.

In the Land of Mystery
there is a Sea of Tranquility,
a place of Rest amidst the wild waters of life.
The waves may be high, our small boat tossed about,
but there we are with a courageous heart.
It is our heart that is courageous.
We are born with this heart.
We do not achieve it.

We can simply rest within our own living heart,
our own courageous heart that opens vulnerably
to every person and all aspects of that person,
to our own self and every aspect of that self,
to life as a whole with all its terrors and joys.

This is a strange Rest, for no storm can end it,
no challenge of life defeat it,
No loss, no death, no horror of being,
no fear can touch our courageous heart.
We live, if we allow ourselves to truly live
on this wild Sea of Everything in the Tranquility
of our own indestructibly courageous heart.

To manifest and fully experience this Tranquility,
we only have to give up the creations of our mind
that we have substituted for this ever-present Peace.
We have only to open to the Land of Mystery
flowing with a River of Consciousness
and containing a Mountain of Care.

Here and here alone do we find the Sea of Tranquility.
Here in the Land of Mystery that our mind
cannot comprehend, create, or control,
here beyond our deepest depth or control
is a Sea of Tranquility
in the Land of Mystery.

PART THREE

The Narratives of Christianity

Parts One and Two of this Book, mentioned Christianity a few times, but my intention in Parts One and Two was to do a discussion of religion in general rather than a witness to the proclamations of the Christian revelation and its practices. I have explored the vast differences of the Eastern religions that tend to focus on getting out of our busy minds into our deep consciousness, while Christianity and Judaism tend to focus on using the mind to build vast narratives that aim to blow our minds into transformations in our views of what is real. I have attempted in Parts One and Two to give respect to both of these relations to the human mind.

One of my favorite Eastern poetic sentences is "Climbing out of the river of thought, I sit by the bank listening." I take that to mean that I allow a detachment from the work of the busy mind and sit in my core consciousness from which perspective I view the works of the human mind as penultimate, while I listen to both that mind at work as well as to those aspects of awareness that the mind cannot probe.

Christianity seeks awareness of a similar import by the creation and telling of narratives—stories, myths, and their interpretations. I will call this "theologizing" rather than "theology," for this Christian witness can never be a static dogma, it must be an ongoing river of thoughtfulness in order to be true to this rather strange heritage that has presented layer upon layer of redone heritage.

I will structure Part Three in four narrative spins

A. The Triune Nature of Awe
B. The Old Testament Stories
C. The New Testament Stories
D. Our Ongoing Story telling

A. THE TRIUNE NATURE OF AWE

WE TYPICALLY USE THE WORD "Awe" in the context of (1) a psychological or contemplative inquiry describing deep states of awareness, having to do with the holy or sacred. There are three overall states of awareness within of the individual human consciousness. (2) We can also meet as holy or sacred conscious references to a more outward Awesomeness that can be an accompaniment of that "objectivity" we associate with the scientific approach to truth. The inward Awe can be viewed as a reflection of this outward Awesomeness. And when the outward Awesomeness is noticed by us, it can be an occasion for the upwelling of Awe within us. (3) A third face of this "Triune Nature of Awe" is the bodily, historical, human beings by whom the Awesomeness is being met and in whom the Awe is upwelling. This thirdness of the Awe experience let us call "the Awed Ones"—such as Abraham, Jacob, Moses, Deborah, Elijah, Isaiah, Jeremiah, and Jesus, Peter, Mary, Paul, and millions more. We have thereby defined three faces of one human event: The Awesome, The Awed Ones, and the Awe itself.

Christianity has structured its thoughtfulness in a manner that is similar to this triune nature of Awe. The Almighty Awesomeness, the Awed humans, and the Holy Awe itself. Christianity follows Judaism in telling of these three faces of the Profound Reality experiences not only from the perspective of key holy individuals but sociologically and historically about communities of persons illuminated by these holy individuals.

For example, the Awe experience can also be seen to be had communally as "the Awed Ones," such as the "resurrected body of Christ Jesus as a historical people, sometimes called "the invisible church." This invisibility does not mean a lack of historical reality. It means that the boundaries of these Awed Ones cannot be identified with the boundaries of the any denominational or sectarian body of Christian practitioners. Muslim, Jewish, Buddhist, Hindu, and other religious practitioners can also be among the Awed Ones who face the Awesomeness and are filled with Awe. All these long lasting religions and a few newer religions can contain members whose non-Christian religious path has opened to them an experience of the Eternal Awesomeness that can happen to any human being anywhere with or without a religious practice.

These inter-religious similarities are being more strongly experienced in our current planetary era. This means new challenges for a next Christian theologizing and some next Christian practices of some next Christian religion that does not confuse its Christian thoughtfulness and its practices with the Awesomeness, the Awed Ones, and the Awe itself—a triuneness that is built into the Profound Reality within which all humans dwell. "I need to make a quick explanation of my use of the word "Awe." I am using it in the more classical meaning as experiences of the "Holy"—that holiness that is both an experience of deep dread as well as deep fascination, and the courage to take on those intensities. That is a deeper meaning than the cheapening of that word we can hear today when someone speaks of "my awesome automobile," or when the word "awesome" is used in response to a payed invitation to a pro-basketball game. Such possibly enjoyable experiences need not be demeaned, but they are seldom probing the experiences of the holy.

More on the Awesomeness

The outward Awesomeness of Profound Reality is met alongside and perhaps through the scientific approach to truth. For example, this massive sphere of rock we call Earth is relentlessly turning slowly one revolution every 24 hours. This means that the surface of the ground at the equator is moving about a 1000 miles per hour from west to east giving we human observers an eastern sun rise and a western sun set, approximately half the time in what we call "day" and half the time in what we call "night." If this powerful Earth turn were not in operation we would have half the planet being cooked by the sun and the other half being frozen by a lack of sun. This also amazing sun is now known to be a hydrogen bomb furnace turning tons of hydrogen into helium and lithium every hour. This furnace is fortunately 93 million miles away from this planet, providing us with temperatures needed for life as we know it. Venice is a plant so close to the son that water would all be steam. Mars is so far from the son that water, if there is any there, would be ice.

We the Earth are rotating around that hydrogen fusion furnace once every 365 earth days. In the temperate zones, because the Earth is tilted in its orbit we have seasons— Spring, Summer, Fall and Winter. At the equator these seasons are so much alike that we temperate zoners would feel them to be as one long summer. At the poles the four seasons are like one long day, Dawn, Day, Dusk and Night. These plain facts of our physical lives are more than simply wondrous. They are Awesome if we allow their reality to Awe us. And the realm of the physical realm continues to amaze us. Our whole solar system is rotating around a black hole in the center of our galaxy so massive that no light can escape from it. And this Milky-way galaxy is one of a hundred billion other galaxies, all of whose origins dates back, at last measure,

13.8 billion years. This vastness borders on the unimaginable, yet we amazing humans do imagine it. And we are only getting started. Our biologies tell us much about the operation of living bodies and their evolution through time, but we still have no clear image of what life is in its relation to the inanimate part the cosmos, or what consciousness is, some measure of which is present in at least in all animal life. And all of this is taking place within a four-dimensional space-time continuum that curves and twists around these huge massive objects in ways that challenge our imaginations..

All this and much more is the cosmos of our human environment of nature that encounters us every moment of our individual and social lives. The Awesomeness of Void experiences, Fullness experiences, and the Total Demand for human response shines through that cosmos (cosmogenesis) to our also mysterious consciousness. In addition, there is our encounter with the environment of our humanly created sociality that is built on top of nature, so to speak, and also within our persons—a social conditioning alongside our biology.

All these sites of the Awesome are expressions of Power—the turn of the Earth, the furnace of he sun, the black hole of the galaxy. the gravitational twists of space time. These powerful encounters mediate the Almighty Power of the Profound Reality that Christian faith trusts with the word "God"—expressing a relationship of devotion, loyalty, and obedience to living the realistic living of our lives in tune with Profound Reality.

More on the Awed Ones

The historical reality of the The Awed Ones appears to us at the boundaries of the interpersonal approach to truth and the commonality approach to truth. In our interpersonal relation, we may find the strange reality of *soul-mates* shinning through the otherwise regular qualities of our interpersonal lives. And in the commonality fabrics of our lives, we may find the Awed Ones with their detachments from their culture, politics and economics moving out into new culture, new polity, new economic life. Every society has these Awed servants creating newness for the whole of group living for That society.

More on the Awe Itself

Finally, we find the Awe itself in our conscious, contemplative inquires into the our own most personal human consciousness. In Chapter 5 of my book *The Thinking Christian*, I have described nine states of this basic Awe:

Trust

> transparent attention - interior alertness
> universal forgiveness - beyond desperation
> effortless letting-be - worldly detachment

Love

> autonomous strength - love of self
> enchantment with being - love of God
> out-flowing compassion - love of neighbor

Freedom

> primal merging - interior initiative
> inherent purity - audacious boldness
> attuned working - obedient liberation

I will not repeat those paragraphs of description here, but only indicate that these qualities of human experience are possible for all humans, including Christians, whom, I believe, have referred to these states as the presence of the Holy Spirit which is viewed as the Spirit of Jesus Christ, as well as the Spirit of the Almighty Profound Reality as well as a Holy Spirit alive within us who allow that holiness to be restored.

So, let this common experience of Awe, sometimes called "wonder," be a metaphorical launch pad for illustrating the universal human quality of a Triune Christian theologizing—three faces (not persons) of thoughtfulness about one overall deep human experience. Let these three faces of Awe be a hint about the faces of Christian theologizing: (1) the Almighty Powerfulness of Profound Reality, (2) the Sons & Daughters of this Almightiness, and (3) the Holy Spirit that drives our theological thoughtfulness and motivates our free agency of witnessing to that Good News love and that justice-seeking love.

B. THE OLD TESTAMENT STORIES

An 8 session introductory course

SESSION ONE

> *In the beginning of creation when God made heaven and earth, the earth was without form and void, with darkness over the face of the abyss, and a mighty wind that swept over the surface of the waters. God said, "Let there be light," and there was light, And God said that the light was good, and God separated light from darkness. God called the light day and the darkness night. So evening came, and morning came, the first day.*

1. The Creation of It All

THE ABOVE QUOTE OF BIBLICAL text is the New English Bible translation of the first paragraph of the Hebrew Bible, called by Christians the "Old Testament"—that is, the old witness to our experience of Profound Reality. The word "God" might also have been translated "Jahweh," the Hebrew personification of the active presence of Profound Reality. Jahweh is being pictured as the Creator of everything. The Creator and the creation is a myth, but the meaning of this "creation story" is not simply about a beginning that set the universe going on its own devices ever after. Rather, Jahweh continues to be the Creator of every moment of our lives today. As John Calvin once humorously put it (I paraphrase), "God gives us the entire universe every morning before breakfast."

Christians in this intensely scientific age have confused this first paragraph of the Bible with science, but if we simply let this paragraph be the first day of a seven-day-structured myth (that is, a story, poem, or fiction), we are engaging this paragraph much more clearly. This poetic piece of writing was put to paper while the Judean exiles were living in Babylon in the sixth century BCE. These two literary sources went into this mythic composition: (1) the seven day calendar of the Hebrew culture and (2) the science of sixth century Babylon.

Notice that the people in that culture in that time and place did not yet connect that the light of the day was coming from the sun, for in this story the sun was not created until the fourth day. Furthermore, no awareness was present in that Babylonian science that the earth was a round ball turning slowly to make night and day in relation to the sun, or that the moon was rotating around the Earth. This first chapter of the Bible was honoring science alright, but it is not the science of educated persons in the 21st century CE. Science is changing. It is still changing. It is the Word of God that does not change. This Word is in the Bible but the words of the Bible are not the Word of God.

The poetry in the above paragraph and the six other paragraphs that follow it are telling us two deep insights about our humanity in relation to nature. (1) that a Profound Reality more powerful than Earth or sun or the whole wonder of nature is creating nature. And (2) that nature is good because this Profound Reality is our God-devotion—the Profound Reality that "does all things well" according to both the Jewish and the Christian saints. Nature is good, however, disagreeable some aspects of nature do not seem good to our ego desires. And our desires, being part of our nature are also good. But the limitations of our desires is also part of nature, or God's creation and therefore good, for all that Profound Realty does is good. That "faith" judges us, we do not get to judge nature or nature's Creator. It is that Enigmatic, Mysterious Profound Reality that judges each and all of us.

Here is a poem I fashioned to illustrate what redoing this ancient poem might look like if we were using a more contemporary science.

> The Infinite Silence spoke
> "Let there be light."
> and the Black Abyss gleamed
> with a single spot
> of trillion-degree illumination,
>
> Expanding where-when
> swirled into being a hundred billion
> galaxies of fiery suns.
> Then super suns exploded
> into super novas of mega-brilliance,
> assembling the elemental parts
> of future planets.
>
> And to the expanded consciousness
> of future beings,
> the Infinite Silence spoke again,
> "All this is good;
> it is very good."

Cascading rocks and ices
sphered themselves into a molten
plasma with gassy skin.
Cooling vapors rained down
oceans upon the rocks and sands
below the bluing skies
of planet Earth.

And the Infinite Silence spoke yet again,
"All this is good;
it is very, good."

Along the beaches of massive oceans,
swamps of thickening chemical soup
assembled the larger molecules
of self-responding beings.

Rods and circles of living substance
exploded into billions of life experiments
along the warmer shores of the waters
that surfaced this sphere of
gas-enveloped
metallic-cored rock.

And the Infinite Silence spoke yet again,
"All this is good;
it is very good."

Life had learned first to fire itself
with decaying complexity,
but soon expanded its grasp to basking in sun rays,

thereby producing the oxygen-enriched air
which life itself was establishing for its
evolution of oxygen breathers.

Multicellular stems and trees of living growths
sprouted up in seas and spread to dry lands.
And as life learned to swim and crawl and fly,
water, land, and air were filled
with interacting forms of living action.

And the Infinite Silence spoke yet again,
"All this is good;
it is very good."

Deep, deep into the calendar of time,
life became aware of being alive,
aware of the destiny of all living beings
the destiny to soon become unalive
and to return again
to the gassy, watery dust.

Self-aware life gazed into the Infinite Silence
into the Dark Abyss,
into the Blazing Fullness of vast and busy interaction,
and self-aware life, filled with dread and fascination,
embraced the courage to hear the Infinite Silence
say once again,

"All this is good;
it is very, very, very good."

SESSION TWO

2. The Poetry of the Psalms

The Book of the Psalms is a collection of Hebrew poetry of a deeply human and religious sort. Many of these Psalms make clear that the Creation was not a once-and-for-all event as our beginning only, but an ongoing process that has never ended. The following verses from Psalm 139:13–18 give us a sense of this everyday reality of the Creator. This psalm is also an exploration of how to use the symbol "Thou" as a devotional word for our relationship with Profound Reality. I have changed a few words in this Psalm to update its meaning for us without changing its original meaning:

> Where can I escape from *Your* Awe?
> Where can I go to flee from *Your* Awesomeness?
> If I climb to the Moon or journey to Mars, *You* are there.
> If I lower my body into my Earthy grave.
> *You* are there as well.

> If I take flight to the edge of the morning,
> or make my home at the far edge of the western ocean,
> even there *Your* handwork grabs me.

> If I say, "Certainly darkness will cover me up, night will conceal me,"
> yet darkness is not dark to *You*.
> Night is as luminous as day
> dark and light are the same for *You*.

It was *You* who fashioned my inward parts;
You knitted me together in my mother's womb.
I praise *You*, because *You* fill me with Awe.
You are wonder-full, and so are *Your* works.

You know me, through and through;
my body is no mystery to *You*,
or how I was secretly kneaded into shape
and patterned in the depths of the Earth.
You saw my limbs yet unformed in the womb
and in *Your* records they were all recorded,
day-by-day they were fashioned,
not one limb was late in growing.

How deep I find *Your* thoughtfulness, O my God!
How inexhaustible are *Your* topics!
Can I count them?
They outnumber the grains of sand!
To finish the count my years would have to equal *Yours*!

This psalmist viewed the Creator creating me in my mother's womb, and is caring for me every day of my life. This psalm gives us a strong vision of the Creator's intimacy with our every-day life rather than only the beginning of the cosmos. Even the current cosmogenesis is all the work of this Creator, all those many billion years of it.

Psalm 90 gives us a different aspect of the Creator's intimacy with us. Here again I am using aa bit of added wording to this Psalm slightly altering for our sensibilities this text from the New English translation without changing its meaning:

Profound Reality has been our place of safety
from generation to generation.
Before there were mountains or the earth or humankind,
Profound Reality was Reality from eon to eon.

Profound Reality turns humankind to dust.
"Turn back to dust" says Profound Reality
to all offspring of the human species.
But for Profound Reality, a thousand years is like a day.
We, however, pass by like a short watch in the night.
We fade to nothing like a dream at daybreak,
like grass which springs up in the morning
and is withered away by nightfall.

It is as if Profound Reality were angry with us.
We are brought to an end.
We are silenced in mid-speech.

Profound Reality lays bare our unrealistic living.
Our desires to be immortal are unmasked as illusions.
As all our days pass by,
each one is marked by this dark shadow of sternness.

Our years expire, each with a deep sigh.
Seventy years is the span of our life,
eighty if our strength holds.

Yet the hurrying years are labor and sorrow.
So quickly they pass and are forgotten.
We who know Profound Reality
are those who also feel Profound Reality's stern
unrelenting power.

So let us allow Profound Reality to teach us,
to count and value each of our days.
Only then, will we feel a heart of wisdom.

I am assuming that the English word "Lord" or the Hebrew word "Jahweh" can be interpreted as Profound Reality, and I am thereby moving this discussion into defining the aim of all the religions on Earth as good if they aid us in our touch with "Profound Reality" Note that it is our ordinary evolutionary evolved natural human consciousness that is being moved into a state of profound consciousness—a life filled with the Awe of this Awesome Profound Reality—filled with the realism of Profound Reality—response-able to act realistically in response to the Ultimate Neighboring of us by this Profound Reality, the Creator of sky and ground.

Psalm 90 is defining Profound Reality using all our human pains, losses, griefs, and disappointments as also characterizing our elemental finite existence. Although such interpretations of the "Divine" is not currently popular in much of the so-called "Christian world," I am going to insist that Jesus' teaching about the arrival of the Kingdom of God are about a happening in human life of the "reign" on Earth in human life of a willing obedience that includes both Psalm 139 and Psalm 90 as essential parts of our view of the Profound Reality awareness we are called to trust and obey as our God.

Some of us have believed or still believe that we have moral values or rational certainties that equip us to judge Profound Reality, this is not in accord with Jewish or Christian faith. It is Profound Reality that judges us, not the other way around. Yes, Profound Reality has given us our passionate cares and is also having them being judged good by Profound Reality that is giving them to us, but this Profound Reality is also giving us limitations to these intense cares. Our desire for security does not end all insecurity. Our desire for pleasure does not end all pain. Our desire for love does not rid us of solitude. Our knowledge is limited. Our actions are undone. Our self esteem can be upended. This is where we find ourselves among those who wish to judge Profound Reality as immoral or not true. Psalm 90 concludes that it is wise for us to trust Profound Reality as trustworthy by us. This trust is an active deed by us humans as being called for by Profound Reality. In other words the Jewish and Christian faith is simply the true deed of realistic living.

Other Psalms elaborate more fully the blessings and bliss aspects of this Profound Reality loyalty and fellowship. I am personally fond of Psalm 23 as an illustration of the blessing or bliss quality of this Profound Reality revelation. Psalm 23 sees a peace, a joy, an equanimity, experienced along with taking in both our welcome gifts and our uphill challenges. Such affirmations of Profound Reality require human freedom. We experience Profound Reality by responding to Profound Reality. Following is Psalm 23 and my commentary on it"

Yahweh is my shepherd. I shall lack nothing.

Yahweh, let us recall, is a not a personification of Profound Reality; it is a personification of our relationship with a Profound Reality that is not in any literal way a shepherd or even "a literal person." Profound Reality is not a big Person, nor big non-Person—not a Rock, not a Foundation, not a Shepherd, not a Fire, not a Spirit, not anything namable by the finite human mind. "Personal" is not a description of Profound Reality— neither "herself," "himself" or "itself." We do not have words that describe the Total Mystery of Profound Reality. All our devotional words for the divine Profound Reality describe our experiences of Profound Reality with out raw human awareness and our response to this Profound Reality with impossible stretches of our limited words. Profound Reality remains wordless to a human being.

142

Even "Eternal Thou" is a projection of our personal relationship with Profound Reality.

Psalm 23 is describing the faith relation with Profound Reality using the poetry of "shepherd and sheep"—"a good shepherd cares for his sheep." That is the metaphor. So here is what Psalm 23 is stating: "The Almighty Profound Reality, that I inescapable confront, is like a shepherd to me; I will not be without everything I really need."

> *[Yahweh] makes me lie down in green pastures*
> *And leads me beside peaceful waters.*
> *[Yahweh] renews life within me*
> *And for "Yahweh's names sake guides me in the right path.*

The first two lines of these elaborating verses remain close to the shepherd metaphor, but with the word "peace" ["peaceful waters with no predators"] this poem reveals that this Profound Reality shepherding is about more than biological food and drink. It is about food and drink for our consciousness of Profound Reality—our equanimity, our authenticity for the realistic living of our lives. The last two verses are quite explicit that we are talking about the inner path toward our authenticity. "For [Yahweh's] names sake" means the reputation of Jahweh—that is, the trust in Profound Reality within human history. The phrase "guides me in the right path" means that Jahweh (the Profound Reality that births us, sustains us, limits us, and ends our lives), also actively clues us about what is authentic living and what is not. Our trusting openness to Profound Reality calls us to realistic living,

With this Psalmist, we are in the "hands" of a skillful poet whose metaphorical creativity is telling us that Profound Reality is in all ways "good" for you and me, a guide for our whole lives. As Julian of Norwich put it, " [Profound Reality] does all things well." In comparison with this Profound Reality who does all things well, our self-created or culturally inherited ideas about good and evil are mostly wrong paths— at best approximate hints. The Psalmist continues this thoroughgoing affirmation by Profound Reality as well as the "goodness" of our return to an affirmation of Profound Reality.

> *Even though I walk through a valley dark as death*
> *I fear no evil, for Thou art with me,*
> *Thy staff and thy crook are my comfort.*

In these verses we are hearing about a "real" experience of Love for our best interests, not a sentimental attempt to view Yahweh as a slave to our ego's shallow wants. The staff of Profound Reality blocks our turn into the perditions of unrealism. The crook of Profound Reality pulls us back into realism. Next the Psalmist moves into the goodness of our affirmative living of each "Living Now":

> *Thou spreadeth a table for me in the sight of my enemies:*
> *Thou hast richly bathed my head with oil*
> *And my cup runs over.*

This extreme confidence of trusting Profound Reality within any situation is said here with remarkable energy. These are ancient metaphors, but they can still "speak" today. These images celebrate the bliss of realistic living. The Psalmist continues with this view of the goodness of Profound Reality and of the life of realistic living:

> *Goodness and Love unfailing, these will follow me all the*
> *days of my life,*
> *And I shall dwell in the house of Yahweh my whole life long.*

It is the "tough love" of Yahweh that is unfailing. The love we think we want, and cook up for ourselves is not unfailing. This Psalm is saying that devotion to Yahweh is my unfailing home port, my father and mother, sisters and brothers. Those who trust the Love of Yahweh are my family. And each of us, whether we know it or not, are essentially sons and daughters of Profound Reality. This response-ability for living a human life can be discovered and learned more about by each of us, in ways that are unique to each of us, yet similar to we humans on every part of this planet, whatever religion they practice or none. Yahweh is always present. Faith is a calling that can happen to us every day. Faith is also our response—a true deed that is intentionally enacted by human awareness and freedom.

Within this context of perpetual care for us by Profound Reality, let us return to the 2nd and 3rd chapters of the book of Genesis—to the myth about our original humanity in our falling away from our realist living of the Profound Reality that created us.

SESSION THREE

3. Adam and Eve
Confessing our Fall

"Confession our Fall" is a sub-title of this story, because I'm going to claim that the authors of the Adam and Eve myth were confessing their departures from Profound Reality—as well as indicating the presence of such departures from Profound Reality by every human being since the beginning of human beings.

This story is about eating the forbidden fruit, from the "Tree of the Knowledge of Good and Evil." This eating is not about a step up—for example the step up from animal consciousness to human consciousness.

Eating this fruit is not about a transformation from a natural awareness to a spiritual awareness . And this story is certainly not about becoming as wise as God, whatever that could possibly mean. In fact, within this story itself "wise like God" is precisely what is forbidden to the human species. Our wisdom is approximate at best. Before the Infinite Reality our wisdom is zero. Our wisdom is not God's wisdom. We are ignorant is a way that cannot be corrected. Being wise, in this story's context, means a surrender to God's wisdom that we can never *understand*.

So, what is this story saying is forbidden to the human by Profound Reality. What is denied to the human is an absolute certainty about what is good and what is evil. This myth also means that the true good is what is Real and that what is evil is what is unreal—a lie, an exaggeration, a misinformation, a false direction for our living. An approximate bit of true knowing is an ambiguous good, for it is approximately *Real* and it is *really* approximate to the good. And because it is approximate, it is also a temptation to evil. Human beings, being finite beings, are always on the razor's edge of realism and a fall into unreality. In fact, growing up in a human culture, we have already fallen into the unrealistic components of that culture. Let us not think of this fall as a simply immorality. The fall is an eclipse of our true being by some moon of our own creation. Our landscape has become dark not because the sun stopped shining, but because we blocked the sunshine.

The delusion that we humans fully know the Real, and thus fully know the Good is the delusion of all delusions. It is this delusion that casts the human out of the Green Garden of Truth into the gray deserts of our false relations with what is Real and true and therefore good.

In other words, the story of Adam and Eve is a confession of your and my departure from our true being:

Our fall from the height of our greatness
Our climb to the sky of our delusion
Our blinding to the truths of our existence
Our eclipse of the sun of our brightness
Our suppression of the moon of our emotional truth
Our twisting of the appropriateness of our responses
Our dulling of the vitality of our aliveness.

This fall from realism is our doing with our Creator-given freedom—that is, freedom at an ontological level of being free or not free. This is not a merely moral level of our response ability. It is a response ability about our choosing of our authenticity.

We hear a lot these days about living in the living Now of our lives, rather than in our fragmentary memories of the past, or in our fragmentary anticipations of the future. We live now; both memory and anticipation are human creations of, in, and by our minds. In each moment of out lives we are tempted to cling tightly to some unreal somewhere—past or future—perhaps a combination of our falsely remembered past and our falsely anticipated future—anywhere but in the living in the now of our ambiguous choices. Let us confess: we all mostly lust for that tree of certainty—that knowledge of good and evil that we can contain is our fragile minds, our finite intuitions, our inherited teachings, our churches' doctrines, our mentors' statements. Our own opinions about the goodness and or the evil of our next choices. Realism means that we live in ignorance—we risk choices boldly and count on forgiveness. We depend on Profound Reality being the Way and Profound Reality's action upon our lives as the clues we need for "goodness and mercy to follow us all the days of our life."

The Adam and Eve story does not condemn our thoughtfulness or our knowledge, but it does condemn our belief that any of our thinking consists of certainty—of being "wise like God." All our thinking yields only approximate knowledge, at best, and foolishness much of the time. Our best physics is approximate knowledge. Our best psychology is approximate knowledge. Our best sociology is approximate knowledge. Furthermore, when we insist on our being the center of value, instead of allowing Reality and realism to be our center of value, we fall from our essence within this goodness of realism. Our commitment to our own preferences over our commitment to realism is far more vast misdirection than we even want to realize or inquire into. We are essentially good beings, yet at the same time we are also fallen beings from our good essence. No rationalist can accept that, so we have to give up our rationalism to be real people. No moralist can accept any of this, so we have to give up our moralism to be real people. No determinist can accept this, for he or she is denying the realism of our freedom to fall or to accept our real freedom or our life devotion to the freedom-giving Profound Reality..

Nevertheless, our knowledge, though not absolute, is approximate knowledge of the One Overall Truth that is coming at us at the speed of time. Although Einstinian physics is approximate knowledge of Profound Reality, it is an approximate knowledge that is a better approximation than the also partially good approximations of Newtonian physics. Knowing that we live within approximations of Reality is realism compared to any of our supposed certainties that we cling to for dear life. Yet the life to which we cling is not so dear as we think, for it is not real and thereby not good, for the good is the real. The real life includes a surrender to our ignorance and our openness to embrace more than we now know. Such openness to the truth is our real life.

We do know such things as the differences between the approximations of our best climate science and what oil company propaganda wants us to accept in our voting practices. We each exist within a great need for confession and forgiveness in the arena of our climate crises underestimations and our neglect of action befitting the challenges of this awesome and grim challenge of climate truth.

We are fighting with God, so to speak, when we deny the approximate truths of the disciplines of learning. Also, we are fighting with God when we deny the approximate nature of the truths that we do know. Fighting with Profound Reality in an appropriate interpretation of all the following metaphors:

> It is eating of the forbidden fruit of good and evil truth.
> It is expulsion from the Green Garden of our realism.
> It is entering the dry deserts East of Eden.

Much more can be said about the stories of Adam and Eve— including the patriarchal obsoleteness of some of the old imagery— such as Eve being visualized as made from a rib taken from Adam, while the truth is that every Adam is born from the womb of an Eve. Nevertheless, the flawed myth of Adam and Eve is revealing to us a very important part in the Genesis introduction to the whole meaning of the Jewish and Christian bibles. We don't get to dismiss the truth of this myth just because all the biblical writers as well as humanity today are not finished with our confession and forgiveness for patriarchy.

The Genesis texts that immediately follow the Adam and Eve story are three well-known stories about estrangement from Profound Reality—Cane's envy crisis with his brother Abel, Noah's flood of wrath on the cities of corruption, the Tower of Babel, a culture built to reach the Eternal sky. These stories tell us more about the wide-spreadedness of the estrangements that follow the fall from realism that the Adam and Eve myth claims were initiated by humanity shortly after our creation.

And the book of Genesis does not end with myths of estrangement the we find in the first 11 chapters. The next set of stories begin with Abram and Sarai becoming Abraham and Sarah, the first parents of our return to Jahweh loyalty. Then we see the stories of Jacob, the schemer, becoming Israel the wrestler with God. Genesis ends with a short novel about Joseph, the overly favored son becoming a wise, firm, tender and responsible head man in Egypt. I will tell these three stories to illustrate the deep faith assumed by the collectors of this Genesis collection of great stories.

SESSION FOUR

4. Abraham and Sarah
First Steps in Realism

While the story of Adam and Eve is about the flight of humanity from realism into a despair-riddled state of affairs poeticized as "East of Eden," the story of Abraham and Sarah is about the human journey toward realism—a dialogue with Profound Reality—a journey of the mind and the feet in companionship with the Ultimate Profoundness they, according to the J writer, named "Jahweh." The beginning of this return to Reality story does not end the story of the fall . Both stories still go on in your life and mine today.

The first step that Abram and Sarai took was to leave hierarchical civilization for the long road to Palestine. They were raised in a city called "Ur," a central city in what is now southern Iraq. They left their parents and siblings and traveled west. They lived in tents and they raised sheep. In his dialogues with Ultimacy, Abram, so the story goes, had heard the promise that he would become in this venture the father of descendants as numerous as the grains of sand on the sea shore.

This adventuresome pair left all their previous lives, not knowing where they were going. They ended up somewhere on the Mediterranean coastal area now called Israel or Palestine. The pair was slow in having children for the promised fatherhood that would entitled Abram to take the name "Abraham." Little did they understand that just continuing this dialogue with Ultimacy was preparing them for this fatherhood.

The myths of Abraham feed off of an actual historical journey of a migrating culture of people in the years following 1800 BCE. These myths of Abraham began to be written up as lasting tradition around 1000 BCE. As mentioned in Part Two of this *Approximate Knowing* book, the Abraham myths pre-suppose and embody a "primal religious metaphor" that characterized that region of the planet long before the Abraham myths were composed and remembered. Important for our current reading, Abraham and Sarah are a myth—a myth about the first parents of the return of humanity to humanity.. Other stories are told about such things, but Jews, Christians, and Muslims all remember Abraham and Sarah and with Islam a bit of action from a mythic character called "Hagar."

The "Abrahamic-Dialogue" metaphor was made from temporal content found mostly from the interpersonal approach to approximate truth—that is, this particular primal religious metaphor that features I-to-I type of relations—person-to-person type of myth about a person to personal relations as well as person to the Profound Reality, creator of sky and ground. The Jewish theologian, Martin Buber, spoke of this as the I-Thou relation and applied his careful thinking to both our person to person human life as well as to our human to the Profound Reality relations of radical realism. The I-Thou myth or poetry is found throughout the Hebrew and Christian scriptures in which we see, first of all, these human conversations of Abram with Yahweh—who is a personification not of Profound Reality but for the human personal relation with Profound Reality. About Profound Reality, remember, we know nothing. That Profound Reality is a person is as untrue as that Profound Reality is a rock. Both "person" and "rock" are metaphors about our relationship with Profound Reality.

In one of his stories Abraham is pictured as having an explicit dialogue with Profound Reality in which Abraham is in an outright bargaining with Profound Reality over how many righteous humans in the horrifically wicked cities of Sodom and Gomorrah it would take to save these cities from their coming destruction. We see Abraham concerned for the lives of his nephew Lot and his family. Abraham talks with Yahweh about all things in his life. Lot and family, you may recall, has to leave those wicked cities. Profound Reality gave Abraham what he gave, not exactly what Abraham bargained for.

Following are two other illustrations of I-Thou dialogues stories.. First, Abraham and Sarah are now past the age of child bearing, but still have no child though which the promise of descendants can be carried out. Then three angel-like men or men-like angels (messengers from Profound Reality) come by their tent in the heat of the day and announced that Sarah was to bear a child. Sarah laughed and Abraham apparently stared in wonder. Sarah did indeed, according to this story, bear a child. This story exaggerates how Isaac was viewed as a miracle child given by Profound Reality, but, if we think about it, this is true of all children. And though all children are the gift of Profound Reality, this child Isaac is being viewed by Abraham as fulfilling the promise made to him by Profound Reality that he is to be the father of descendants as numerous as the grains of sand on the sea shore.

The next Abraham story that I am going to cite has had whole books written about it. Both theologians and philosophers have argued about it until the present day. Like the other stories, this preposterous story is a myth shaped with the ancient I-Thou-relation primal religious metaphor. In this story, Abraham in his ongoing conversations with

Profound Reality becomes aware that all the gifts from Profound Reality have to be given back to Profound Reality, including the gift of Isaac that is so central to Abraham's whole life. Abraham sees this awareness of giving back as his own command to be the very knife that gives Isaac back. So he proceeds to make this sacrifice.

This story seems outlandish, but let us notice that it is true that all parents have to give back their children to Profound Reality—if not with the death of their children, then within their children's life time to face the simple fact that their children will grow up and go about their own lives. This entails a type of giving-them-up that challenges all parents. Abraham grasps somehow that not clinging to Isaac is part of his Profound-Reality dialogue.

In the completion of this strange story, Profound Reality appears to say to Abraham with the appearance of a goat trapped in the next bush, "OK you have done the command of giving up Isaac, I am providing you the goat in yonder bush for your symbol of this needed sacrifice. Abraham grasps this as Profound Reality doing a re-giving of Isaac to be his hope of continuing the promise of Profound Reality for numerous descendants.

As we look back on this story in the context of an I-Thou dialogue with Profound Reality, we see that this *giving back to the Giver of our gifts given by the Giver* is the seed that Abraham is passing along to so many other humans. Abraham's descendants are those who live out "*the spirit seed of giving back all gifts to the Giver.*" The Genesis and Exodus stories continue this narrative of such descendants coming to pass through Isaac, Jacob, Joseph, Moses, and an ongoing mighty chorus of Jewish, Christian and Islamic religious practitioners (women and men) who came to see and still see Abraham as their spirit ancestor. This seed does indeed still live in the millions.

In this 21st century CE, the women are fleshing out the role of Sarah in these old stories that have neglecting her role in this adventurous parenting. Sarah is the first mother of the People of God. She, not only Abram, left Ur not knowing where she was going. She bore Isaac, she shared the whole story. We have forgotten her to much in this long patriarchal period.

5. Jacob
Wrestling with the Profound

Jacob takes on the seed of the realistic living of giving back our gifts to the Giver. With Jacob this seed of Abraham begins to grow a tree that takes in Profound Reality and puts forth obedience to Profound Reality. Abraham was an exodus from the unrealism of putting forth our own reality and expecting others to obey that. Jacob dramatizes how taking in Profound Reality more deeply and putting forth obedience to Profound Reality more specifically involves major transformations in your life and in doing that hard careful work of living realistically.

Jacob, having cheated his brother Esau and fooled his father Isaac with help from his mother Rachel, is now at about the age of 16, let us say, fleeing alone on foot from the wrath of his brother and father on his way to the house of his uncle Labon with only a rod of protection and some sandwiches to eat. The first night out, while sleeping with a rock for his pillow, he has a vivid dream about a staircase or ladder extending to the top story of Reality. In this dream Jacob hears again the promise made to Abraham. The next morning he made a pact with "the God of his fathers" to devote himself and his gifts back to the Giver, if he could just be kept safe until he got to Laban's house. So in this personally intense way, Jacob became the custodian of the Abrahamic legacy.

Isaac was not a very good father. He favored one son over the other. Perhaps he thought Esau would be a better carrier of the Abrahamic faith. The storytellers also suggest that Isaac identified more with Esau's hairy outdoor ruggedness than with Jacob's more smooth-skinned body and scheming thoughtfulness. Rebecca (and Reality too, apparently) disagreed with Isaac. As this unusual biblical story goes, the woman character had a better grasp of Reality than the man had. With help from Rebecca, Jacob tricked Isaac out of a blessing intended for Esau. The story proceeds with Jacob carrying on the Abrahamic legacy. Herein is a lesson for us: *We never know what Profound Reality will do, or who Profound Reality will choose to do what.*

Laban had two daughters: Rachel, whom Jacob dearly loved, and Leah, whom Laban tricked Jacob into marrying first, and then working another seven years for Rachel. Years later, Jacob left Laban, taking his two wives, many children, and a big flock of sheep that Jacob had "fleeced" out of Laban. On his way, he learns that he was going to intersect with his estranged brother coming his way with three hundred men. So this was the night for his all-night wrestling match with an angel of Profound Reality. He persisted in this struggle until he was given a new name "Israel," which means "striver or struggler with Yahweh." The next morning Jacob arose limping because of a dislocated hip to met Esau. His old name "Jacob" was associated with the life style of "trickster." So this event was a massive repentance and a fresh start.

This fresh start was dearly needed to met Esau. With Jacob's diplomatic realism in full operation, he made friends with Esau, and then got on his way before Esau changed his mind about fighting him. This is a story worthy of many sermons that I will not include. The main point of this story is that Jacob found his essential freedom that he then used to talk carefully with his brother—giving up his old trickster lifestyle and taking on the wrestling-with-God life style of "Israel"—one who strives with Profound Reality and thereby wins realism for a new life.

So Jacob's "biblical sainthood" means seeing yourself out of control by a Mystery you don't understand, and yet seeing yourself responsible for everything that happens in your life. His Genesis sainthood means to us seeing ourselves in a dialogue with a Powerful Infinity greater than us, and yet seeing and obeying that Reality as a friendly Power that is giving us the freedom that we can then use with all our alertness in choosing our still unknown and constantly re-decided destiny.

6. Joseph
Gifts used by the Gifted

Like Abraham and Jacob, Joseph is a narrative about more than it seems. It is clearly not a scientific biography of an actual historical personage or about what really happened or even what might have happened. It is also something more than an unusually good historical novelette tacked onto the end of the book of Genesis. So what is this story about?

It is indeed a novelette that references historical realities, but it is more. It is "holy scripture" in the following way: Joseph is the seed of Abraham. He is the character in a fictional story about the essence of giving back all your gifts to the Giver. His story is a narrative about the nature and role of the People of God. He is (hold your credulity for this) the true church, the Body of Christ, the Word of God, the communication of the Almighty operating in an imaginary view of historical moments, each filled with possibilities.

So what are the details? Joseph is the 11th of 12 sons of Jacob. He is the most gifted of the twelve. His father adores and favors him. His younger brother looks up to him. His oldest brother is proud of him and protects him from the envy and jealousy of the other 9 brothers. And Joseph is the first son of Jacob's favorite wife Rachel.

In this story the envy-afflicted 9 brothers find an opportunity to kill him, but the eldest brother scales that down to throwing him into a pit. The eldest brother intends to come back and rescue him. But before he can return to do that, some greedy scoundrels come by and sell Joseph into slavery.

His owner is soon impressed with him, for Joseph uses his gifts to become a very good slave. Even the owner's wife falls for him and gets him in trouble with her husband who then puts him in jail. In jail he makes friends with a servant of the Pharaoh of all of Egypt. That servant of the Pharaoh has a disturbing dream which Joseph, with his vast sensitivities, interprets so helpfully that when the Pharaoh has a disturbing dream, this servant tells the Pharaoh about Joseph, who is then called before Pharaoh to interpret his dream.

The Pharaoh's dream is about cows (eight cows fat and then eight cows lean). Joseph sees in this dream some sociological meaning for Pharaoh's responsibility. There will be eight years of plenty followed by eight years of famine in that whole Mediterranean corner. This sensible Pharaoh sees that he must launch an emergency program of saving grain during the period of abundance for the coming lean period, and he puts Joseph to work on that project.. Joseph is so good at everything he does, that he is appointed head person in the administration of this project.

At the end of the eight years of plenty, Joseph's father and brothers who are living back in Palestine come into severe want. So Jacob sends his elder 10 sons to Egypt to buy and bring home a large supply of grain. Jacob keeps his twelfth son, Benjamin, home, because he does not want to lose Rachel's second son, like he lost Joseph. This is where the story takes on the high points of the novelist's art. Joseph is the one who is negotiating with his brothers for the grain. They do not realize that this Egyptian executive is their brother, and Joseph does not tell them yet. He forces them to bring their younger brother Benjamin back with them for their next trip. Then, he keeps Benjamin as a hostage to force bringing back their aging father Jacob, who is also called Israel. With the whole family of patriarchs there, he then reveals himself, works through a reconciliation, forgives his guilty brothers, explaining that "what they meant for evil, God meant for good."

The whole clan is then moved to Egypt where Joseph can support them. Their descendants prospered until there came into being an Egyptian administration that "knew not Joseph."

This brief retelling of the story is perhaps enough to make a few general comments about the Joseph character. He is a portrait of the nature of the presence of the people-of-God. He is a story about a personage who is giving his gifts back to the Giver, and he is doing so with competence in whatever situation that the Giver is giving to Joseph—a situation of favoritism, mistreatment, slavery, prison, opportunity, success, estrangement, responsibility, reunion, emotional intensity, whatever.

Here is a second generalization dramatized by this character Joseph: Being the people of God does not only mean a solitary state of being; it also means a sociological responsibility. In fact, being the people of God is a key dynamic in making truly progressive steps in world history, as well as such steps in our personal lives.

Laying down your life and all your gifts in whatever situation you are facing is the life style that defines who are the people of God. The New Testament Gospel portraits of Jesus and his spirit descendants provide a companion story to this old portrait of Joseph. Jesus' "revelation" shows us that "unto death" can mean unto death in a most grueling fashion. At the same time, Jesus' intentional dying became a pathway toward the birth of a whole new family of radicals who manifested Jesus' same full manner of detachment and engagements on behalf of all humankind and their planet—doing so with all their gifts in the situations being given to them.

To those of us who allow ourselves to hear these stories deeply, they call to us to be the Joseph people, the Jesus people of God—the loyalists of Yahweh who is a personification or our relation with the Profound Reality of the whole cosmos.

SESSION FIVE

7. Moses and Joshua

Moses and Joshua are not pure myth like Adam and Eve or simply a character in a short novel like Joseph. Moses is a real historical figure whose historicity is so overlaid with legend and exaggerated story-telling that the historical man almost disappears from view. The same is true of Joshua. Moses led the Exodus escape around 1290 BCE,, according to some scholars, and that would mean being the religious leader, politician, and military leader of this group of ex-slaves in a wilderness fit only for goats for the next 40 years.

After Moss's death the leadership of this now stronger body fell to Joshua.who was probably born during those 40 year in the wilderness with Moses. Following is my short story of the lives and meanings of those two memorable figures. I am going to tell these very old stories in my own plausible way. The biblical accounts of these events were first written down for us after 990 BCE—at least 300 years after the Exodus, and then these stories were rewritten many more times for another 300 years or so. The originating events were elaborated in narratives quite beyond what is plausible for we scientific historians living today.

Moses

the Law-giver for Yahweh

Moses was a religious man in a culture of slaves who may have remembered some very early stories about Abraham, Isaac, and Jacob. Moses had fled to the outback to live with a relative after having killed an Egyptian soldier who was mistreating a fellow Hebrew slave. Herding sheep one day, he found his whole vocational life set on fire—a fire that burned hot, but did not consume. This is the essence of the experience told in that burning-bush story. We modern interpreters know that this bush burning was most likely a projection on that bush of a fire burning in Moses own life, concerning the horrific call to lead his people from their slavery.

It is probable that such an interior burning resulted is the transformed life that enabled Moses (with help perhaps from his brother who spoke more fluidly) to inspire a group of Egypt-enculturated slaves to pick up their babies, some swords, and a few possessions and wade across some waters in which the chariots that sought to stop them got bogged down, allowing these slaves to escape into the wilderness. Other slaves had also escaped. Many tries had not. But Moses saw and taught that this event showed the power of a freedom giving Profound Reality. We, so he said, have the freedom to change our history. Let us not forget this revelation of Profound Reality's kindness towards us.

It was in this wilderness, a land good only for goats, that Moses became a statesman, a religious leader, and probably a military organizer with usual skills that served these people for the next 40 years. Here is how that story goes.

At Mount Sinai Moses, the lawyer, got underway. I picture Moses holding up two hands indicating 10 mandates for law writing. We don't know the exact form for those first 10 teachings, for Exodus 20 was written in the form we now read it at least 300 years later. We can guess, however, that Moses did inspire a style of law-writing that was different from the Egyptian autocracy, a law-writing that did not end with Moses, but took place during the next 600 years or more of Old Testament formation. Nevertheless, let us imagine the following story of those Sinai moments.

In his left hand, let us say, Moses enumerated five mandates for his ongoing Exodus law writing that fostered maintaining obedience to that Final Profound Reality that grants history-making freedom to human beings:

Here is my wording for these five mandates:

1. Have no other loyalties beyond this final loyalty to Profound Reality.
2. Create no earthen facsimiles for this Mysterious Wholeness.
3. Use even the name "Yahweh" with care.
4. Keep one day out of seven for holy ritual and rest.
5. Honor your ancestry in this holy covenant.

With his right hand, I am picturing Moses enumerated five more mandates—this time for getting along with one another in order to survive this wilderness and defend against the other groups who are also trying to make it in this forbidding environment. Here's my wordings for these five mandates:

1. Don't kill each other.
2. Don't steal from each other.
3. Don't violate someone else's spouse.
4. Don't bear false witness in the courts of justice.
5. Don't crave some other person's life over your own life, live creatively the life that Yahweh, our deliverer, has given to you.

Moses began his work as a lawyer with a rag-tag Egyptian-enculturated mob of desperate slave families. After 40 years in this wilderness, he had inspired and trained a much larger and stronger body of persons who were living the Mosaic breakthrough in realism and courage for responding to Profound Reality.

What actually transpired at Sinai we do not know, but we can guess what was launched there was more important than a final set of specific laws that some modern Christian moralist can post on the base of a state monument.

The 10 commandments are best understood as 10 mandates for on-going law writing—law writing that obeys the Profound Reality that we humans meet in each new situation of our actual lives. The history of the writing of the Old Testament texts witnesses to that understanding of a long law-writing period. Each generation of Bible writers "raised Moses from the dead" (So to speak) to write new laws relevant for each new time. They kept within the original mandates, but they obeyed the changing times that Yahweh was understood to be bringing to them for their responding. Law-writing was part of their ongoing responding to the action of Yahweh (Profound Reality) in the present historical needs for new laws. We can still do that sort of law-writing in our own political and ecological situations.

The Mosaic core style of doing "lawful" thoughtfulness would last within all three of these significant religious branches: Judaism, Christianity, and Islam. Moses affected law-writing from about 1290 BCE until 2024 CE, at least 3314 years,. The lucid and persistent followers of Moses have impacted history for the betterment of all humankind all that time. I am not talking here about the corrupt forces within all three of these religions. I am talking about those "people of God" who were responding to Yahweh, to Allah, to the Lord God Almighty in their actual situations. I am talking about both the prominent and the unremembered leadership in realistic living who gave social order to generations of people in the wake of Moses.

We can understand the Exodus events as a revelation of the mercy of the Absolute Mystery of Profound Reality that actually confronts us in every moment of our lives with possibilities for better arrangements and for the happiness in bringing those better arrangements into being. Following are aspects of the lasting truth about law-writing that was revealed in the Exodus events and by their followers.:

1. Each specific enforceable law is written by temporal humans, not by the agency of some divine being. Yet the Exodus also reveals that these humanly-written laws can be written in obedience to the Final Profound Mysterious Reality that we all face every day of our lives. We do not live without laws. Law restrains our fallen impulses, narcissistic egoisms, self-promotion exaggerations, and down-right wickedness.

2. These social laws provide a social environment that we all share along with our natural environment. The difference between these two complimentary environments is the way in which humans are responsible for having created our social environment and are responsible for creating the next social environment. We humans are not the creators of the natural environment, even though we are part of it, and our actions impact the nature of it in ways we intend and do not intend. We humans are the creators of our social environment and are each and all responsible for the future of this environment for all of us. Care for our neighbors includes care for the social environments in which we live and in which our descendants will live.

3. It is in and through the ongoing historical events within these two environments (natural and social) that we encounter the God of Moses—that Mysterious Profound Reality that no generation of us can escape.

4. There are many ways to organize our natural environmental care and our social environmental justice; however, helter-skelter is not the best way. Today a fully democratic politics is a better way to order society than the ways that the supposed "strongmen"—such as Trump, Putin, etc. have figured out. We can discern with our own eyes that the wisdom of the whole group, accurately expressed, is a wiser arbiter than any mighty few who make choices first of all for the satisfaction of their own foolish and greedy egos and for the revengeful ruin of those who oppose them, and in consequent neglect of the issues that affect us all.

5. We Exodus-awake citizens, without aspiring to be perfect, can take on the Exodus challenge to organize fellow citizens of our own nations of people—whatever their face color and happiness preferences—to the end that everyone is provided "life, liberty, and the pursuit of happiness." This has been tested. It works. And we neglect it to our serious pains of social oppressions from which our deliverance may be difficult.

So, if we can think these democratic thoughts, we can surely attempt their realization. We don't have to give-in to the patterns of "winner takes all" monopoly games in our economics or to give in to an ethical philosophy of "I-can't-do-anything" excuse making in our politics and culture. The Exodus possibility and challenge is this: realism-loving humans have the freedom to change the course of history, and to do so toward a better realism. And we have in the biblical record centuries of life experience about how that can be done.

The Exodus is about compassionate action in comradeship with a confidence in the merciful Profound Reality that is giving us the freedom that is also our hope for an optimal future in this real world.

After the death of Moses, a second Exodus-spirited leader, Joshua, organized a conquering army and their families to move across the river Jordan into a "promised land" of more fertile ground—flowing with milk and honey (cows, flowers, and bees).

Joshua
Conquering a New Home for the Moses Breakthrough

Joshua gathered some, perhaps not all, of the Moses clan at the river Jordan and spoke to them about a new covenant for a new life in a land flowing with milk and honey. This "promised land," however, was already occupied by numerous other tribes waring with each other in an un-pretty way, so this will be a hard conquest and living on a constant war footing for centuries to come. This place had long been known by spying visits by some of the Exodus people, but no movement into it could be contemplated until they were numerous enough and strong enough in spirit to see success within such a change of life.

No one could have predicted how brutal and how hard this was going to be. But this people did manifest military strength enough and spirit enough and were imaginatively organized well enough under a body of "Mosaic Judges." These judges were military leaders as well as interior conflict resolvers. Incredibly, one of these judges, Deborah, was a women, and reputed to be a strong military leader as well as a wise conflict resolver.

Those who give Joshua a hard time for his military brutality, need to also understand that if Joshua's definiteness and courage and thoughtful contextual ethics choices had not happened, we would never have heard of the Moses Exodus, nor of the Prophets, nor of Jesus. The Joshua style of realistic living lasted 300 years before the choice to have a King who might organize life better was opted for. The first King Saul was a good military man but a poor king. A guerrilla leader named "David" pulled off a conquest from within Saul's first rickety kingdom. David turned out to be the model for a "good king." According to his legacy, he was a strongly religious man, a musician, a poet, a liturgist, and probably a sponsor of the biblical text writer we call "J." David and his kingdom has been accused of not even existing, because his life was so overlaid with legend and because his kingdom left no archeological ruin.

But the stories of David are so vivid, and not all complementary of David, that a real human being is plausible to me. It is probably that the story of his slaying the giant Goliath with a sling shot and with Goliath's own sword was fiction. This story was, nevertheless, one of the first Bible texts that lured my own boyhood. There is a courage and an excellence expressed in David's whole story about his alive realism and improbable success of that early kingdom. Also David's repentance though Nathan's trickery about David having gotten a soldier killed so David could marry his beautiful wife, Bathsheba, shows David to be both a typical ancient monarch, and yet something more flexible than the common run of kings.

SESSION SIX

8. The Axial Prophets of Israel and Judea

The religion of Israel and Judea came to its International sophistication along with the Buddha, the Upanishads, Lao Tzu, Confucius, and Zarathustra. The Hebraic luminaries of this period were at least Amos,

Hosea, Isaiah, Jeremiah, Ezekiel, and Second Isaiah. I will tell each of their stories briefly to conclude this survey of Old testimony stories upon which the New testimony of stories are built. My story telling of these figures are built with my study of their historical situations and my attempt to resonate existentially with their responses to their challenging times.

Amos
Let Justice Roll

Amos is not a mythic person or a legion from the deep past. He is a real human being whose written words we still have—words that have been copied all these centuries since before 800 BCE. Amos is the first of the Axial Hebrew prophets who brought the religion of Israel and Judea into its mature state that we find in most of the Old Testament writings.

Amos viewed himself as a messenger of Yahweh bringing Yahweh's address to the northern kingdom of Israel, just before the Syrian conquest of that nation. Amos addressed their delusions of safety and their delusions of righteousness. He pointed out their unrighteousness along with that of the nations around them in their international scene. He began one of his speeches asserting Yahweh's judgement on those surrounding nations for whom judgement was easy to hear by the people of Israel. Then Amos moved his attack to Judea, their sister nation to the south, and then to their overconfidence, unrighteousness and vulnerability of the northern kingdom of Israel to whom Amos was speaking. If we were to give an Amos-like address to the people of the United States in our historical situation, it might sound something like this:

"Hear the message of Truth form Profound Reality: For three estrangements and for four of the terrorist networks of global scope, I will not withhold my wrath, for they have taken the lives of innocent men, women and children, bombed embassies, and flown commercial airlines into occupied buildings. I will hound them and chase them until their networks are broken to pieces, their training camps are laid in waste, and their bank accounts emptied. Suicidal terrorism will become the butt of jokes about moronic behavior. This is the Truth, the speech of Profound Reality."

And then this Amos-like prophet for today would move to Putin's Russia and other places of obvious estrangements that most US citizens can still easily judge. Then he would focus his attack on Canada and Mexico, and finally on the United States of America. Amos would present to the United States some understanding of their vulnerabilities and their estrangements. Here is how that might sound:

"For three estrangements and for four of the United States of America, I will not withhold my wrath. Decade after decade the US has assisted in the overthrow of legitimate and popular elected national leaders, replacing them with dictatorial thugs who were willing to do the bidding of greedy corporations. In pursuit of these ends the US has directly or indirectly caused the deaths of millions of innocent men, women, and children.

"The US spent billions of your tax dollars on costly wars to preserve your oil addictions, while refusing to invest strongly in moderating the climate emergency. This nation has promoted and allowed in the US and the planet drastic racial and economic inequities. For the women of the world, you have been unwilling to liberate them from their second state status. The media, educational, and religious institutions have reduplicated these failures of racism, homophobia, patriarchy, triviality, sloth, insane addictions, and needless violence.

"Therefore, will I increase the anger against you in all the hopelessly poverty-stricken places. There will be further terrorism. The oceans will arise and drown your coastal cities. The weather patterns will turn your crop lands into deserts, Your rivers will become sewers. I will push your economy to the worst recession it has ever known,

"Do you indeed long for the day of justice, the day of Yahweh, the day of Truth. That Grand Day will be darkness and not light for you. It will be as when a man runs from a lion and has a bear meet him. He turns into a house and leans his hand against the wall and has a snake bite him. The day of Justice will indeed be darkness and not light for you, a day of gloom with no dawn.

"I hate your prayer days and your flag waving ceremonies. Spare me the noise of your patriotic songs. I cannot stand another verse of America the Beautiful. But let justice roll down like water and righteousness like an ever-flowing stream."

A paraphrase of Amos 5:24 to. 6:17

Hopefully, some of the disasters suggested in this hastily written poetry will not come to pass, for choices remain to be made that may evoke a different response from Reality. The words of a possible prophet may not be accurate predictions of the future. The intent of the prophet is to move listeners to an awareness of the choices that we face in the present. Amos gives us a sense of how that can be done.

Hosea
Forgiveness for the Wayward

The prophet, Hosea, addresses Israel a few years later than Amos when the Assyrian conquest is further along and the illusory confidence of the nation of Israel has been shaken. The nation's unrighteousness is now being more fully acknowledged. It has become a time in which the Israel society at large is having feelings of hopelessness and futility.

Hosea does not take back the stern judgment of Profound Reality that Amos has announced upon the over-confidence of a nation not facing the reality it was confronting. But now, Hosea is speaking words of forgiveness and a fresh start for the survivors of this horrific tragedy that is well underway.

Hosea likens Israel to an unfaithful wife who, though deserving complete rejection, has been experiencing a period of tough training, and is now being offered restoration to full standing as wife of the household—in this metaphor Israel remains the household of the Almighty Awesomeness who rules the course of history.

Hosea also likens Israel to a child whom this Awesome Yahweh has raised since the days of the Exodus—a child that God loves and will not abandon to complete doom. Hosea is confronting his listeners with an Awe-filling choice—rather than (1) give up and die out as the people who revere Yahweh, they can (2) accept the challenge of receiving the gift of forgiveness and begin again to build continuity within the Mosaic breakthrough.

In order to hear Hosea's voice speaking into our situation today, we might recall what it felt like in the 1960's of our US history. when Martin Luther King Jr. was a voice of hope in relation to the established racism that at the time seemed almost impossible to break. For those of us who are African American, or are identified with the African American oppression, Martin King's dream at that time was like a bright light of hope, shining in a very dark place.

A sermon given at that time by James Bevel, one of King's associates, spoke a message similar to Hosea's . The title of his sermon and of a repeated line spoken again and again throughout that grim, but hopeful talk was "Love can find a way!"

Hosea and Bevel may be the right prophet for today as we face the gloom and doom of the Disunited States of America. We need to hear again (1) Hosea telling us about forgiveness and a fresh start, (2) King dreaming dreams of justice, and (3) Bevel telling us that "Love can find a way through and beyond the current conditions !

Love in this context is an active doing of our whole lives, not a passive sentiment of comfortable escape from reality. It is this sort of love that can vigorously put down the enemies that are destroying our nation. It is Jahweh's stern way of love that serves all types and states of people. It is an empathetic sort of love that pays attention to everyone in this tough time of life, and it is those who listen to the prophets of old and allow their motivating imagery to inspire our living.

Love is a human essence that we don't have to create. It is a deep mountain of care within each of us. It is love for whatever and whoever neighbors us. It is the love that remains when all our foolishness, self-promotion, and lies are relinquished to the Truth of our real situation and our true capacity for a loving response..

And such love is aware that human social life is not something inevitable that is going to work out OK without human response-ability making good choices. Nor is human social life a state of things set in an everlasting fate. Choices can make everything much worse. And choices can make everything much better. "Love can find a way!" Hosea wrote his love song for an extreme moment for a whole nation of his people who still carried those ancient Mosaic gifts of trust in a trustworthy and forgiving Overall Reality.

Isaiah
Advisor of Realism

I'm still grateful to Bernard Anderson and his book *Understanding the Old Testament* for helping me see the prophets in their historical settings. The prophets were not magical predictors of the future, nor moralistic preachers, but interpreters of the historical events of their times.

The prophets were listeners to the "speech" that the Awesome Wholeness was "sounding" to them through their historical events. Then the prophet speaks in powerful verse to his or her social companions. Prophets speak what they have heard being "said" by the Awesome Wholeness about their historical encounters. At the same time a prophet knows that this Mighty Awesomeness is always saying more than any human can discern.

Here is a rough summary of the historical situation to which Isaiah was speaking. The Assyrian empire had already defeated the Northern Kingdom of Israel and was on its way to challenge Egypt to the south. The Assyrian leaders, wished to control the lucrative trade routes down the eastern coasts of the Mediterranean Sea—thus passing through the northern kingdom of Israel, and through the outskirts of the southern mountain kingdom of Judea.

Against Isaiah's advice, the frighted king of Judea made a covenant of defense with Egypt. This made even more likely an Assyrian army's stopover for a conquest of Jerusalem. Speaking for Yahweh, Isaiah penned these words:

> *Ah! Assyria the rod of my anger,*
> *the staff of my fury.*
> *Against a godless nation I send him,*
> *and against the people of my wrath I commanded him*
> *to take spoil and seize plunder*
> *and tread them down like mire in the streets.*

Then speaking of Assyria, Isaiah continues:

But he does not does not so intend,
and his mind does not so think.
But it is his mind to destroy.
and to cut off nations not a few.

Then speaking as himself, Isaiah says:

When Yahweh has finished all his work
on Mount Zion, and on Jerusalem,
he will punish the arrogant boasting of the king of Assyria
and his haughty pride.

. . . . . .

Shall the axe vaunt itself over him who hews with it?
Or the saw magnify itself against him who wields it?
Isaiah 10:5-7, 12, & 15 of the Revised Standard Version

Isaiah sees history, as a drama in which the God he worships is actively present in every event. The Assyrian conqueror does not know he is a rod in God's hand. It is Isaiah who has this wider view of history. The Profound Reality that Isaiah calls "Yahweh, his God" is none other than the awesome Finality that is present and operative in every historical event. This Mysterious Reality is an encounter through the events of the natural environment and also through the events of the social environment. This statement does not deny the freedom of Isaiah or the freedom the Assyrian leadership. Yahweh grants freedom to human beings, and thus humans bear responsibility for their actions.

Isaiah's God is not a magical protector of the interests of Isaiah's nation. Yahweh is the operative Truth arriving to audit Isaiah's own nation for its shoddy living, for its delusions, and lack of trust in Yahweh—that is, its trust in the trust-worthiness of the Profound Reality being faced.

This Assyrian leader thinks himself something he is not, in charge of social history.

History is ruled by a much more powerful Reality. Isaiah is making clear that he and his people are confronting their life choices within a much bigger context than the world politics of the Assyrian strategists.

So how does this story work out. A very large Assyrian army is surrounding the walled city of Jerusalem and calling for the king to be cast over the walls. Perhaps the Assyrian general hoped not to waste a single soldier on this insignificant place. Isaiah counsels not to give up their king, just to wait. They do wait and wait and wait and wait.

Finally, the Assyrian general just leaves. Perhaps he has no more time to use on this little kingdom. Perhaps he has received information of a bigger crisis. Perhaps he was just tired of dealing with this stubborn people and their patient courage.

Many people of Judea came to believe that Yahweh would never allow Jerusalem to fall. In Jeremiah's day, however, that turned out to be wrong. Jeremiah was a prophet in the time of the Babylonian conquest that carried off the leadership of Judea into exile where they waited on Yahweh for almost 5 decades before they were allowed to be led home to Judea by a disciple of Isaiah that scholars have called "2nd Isaiah" because his writings were recorded on the scroll of Isaiah.

As the above words of 1st Isaiah strike contemporary ears, we who fight for democracy and an ecologically sane planet can find encouragement in the wider context that Isaiah spins. So viewing our 21st Century times, we might be able to see that Putin and Trump are only rods in the hands of Yahweh sent to our sleeping and illusion-drenched democracies to awaken them from their unrealism and to summon them to the roadways of realism, repentance, and response—actions that keep the faith that our loyalty is to no ecstatic egotistical leader, but to the Profound Reality that always wins in the end. So may we indeed wait upon Profound Reality to renew our strength and to find our ways of response-ability through sober dealing with the challenges that we face?

SESSION SEVEN

Jeremiah
Covenant of the Heart

The stories, writings, and wisdom of these Old Testament prophets (at least, Amos, Hosea, Isaiah, Jeremiah, Ezekiel, and Second Isaiah) compare in depth with the authors of the Upanishads and the Buddha in India, Lao Tzu and Confucius in China, Zoroaster in Persia, and other luminaries living in this same basic time period—a period named by Karl Jaspers the Axial Period (roughly 800- 500 BCE—perhaps until 322 if we include Socrates, Plato, and Aristotle). These centuries are a time of spirit deepening and Reality expanding—a revolution in inwardness as well as a wider perspective that transformed the earlier forms of civilization all across much of the planet.

In these so-called Axial years, these earlier civilizations underwent a deep critique by a very fresh perspective. We can generalize the essence of this widespread social shift—"a deeper consciousness" about profound solitude and about the historically faced Profound Reality that stretched the rigid clinging of these early civilizations that were being conducted by the pre-Axial style of civilization. The early civilizations were uniform, closed systems of narrowly permitted thought and action. These Old Testament prophets accomplished for the people of Moses the kind of deepening that these other luminaries did of other geographies. Such deepening had historical ramifications in many directions and for hundreds of years following. To these spirited explorers, we owe a debt of gratitude for our understanding of the autonomous power of the individual person and for our capacities for maintaining an ongoing critique of our cultural configurations. We can fight for our own deep experiences rather than bow to the decayed traditions, These luminaries also revealed the presence of that Profound Reality that is more than the contents of our human-made cultural canopy.

Jeremiah is a vivid example of all this axial prophetic power. He is living at the time of the conquest of Judea by the Babylonian Empire and the complete destruction of Jeremiah's home nation making Judea a puppet of Babylon.. The elite population was being carried off into exile in Babylon. Jeremiah, facing these grim events, spoke of a new covenant with Profound Reality—one "written on our hearts." That message included the deep awareness that losing the nation as the historical manifestation of Mosaic peoplehood was not the end of being "the People of God"—the ones devoted to the One Profound Reality. The role of this people in history could be carried on as exiles in Babylon. Jeremiah, in spite of being an interpreter of an extremely grim social situation, was an incredibly optimistic voice—in addition to facing up to the obvious grimness that few wanted to take in, Jeremiah proclaimed a deep quality of hope. This hope had an Axial Period quality that was lived on in Babylon captivity with help from Ezekiel and others. When the Persian conquests allowed exiles to return to their homelands, these exodus people in exile were inspired by Second Isaiah to return to Palestine as rebuilders of a fresh Israeli nationhood and its ancient mission to the world.

Also, the Babylonian exile was not a period of religious vacuum for these exiles. Most likely the first chapter of the Bible was written there. Certainly many of the psalms express that "covenant of the heart"— the personally deep impulse given by Jeremiah and others. Following is some of that new-covenant-style Old-Testament poetry from Psalm

139:13–18. I am using the New English Bible, reworded a bit by me. This psalm is also an exploration of how to use the symbol "Thou" or "You" as a devotional word for our relationship with Profound Reality.

> *It was You who fashioned my inward parts;*
> *You knitted me together in my mother's womb.*
> *I praise You, because You fill me with Awe.*
> *You are wonder-full, and so are Your works.*
> *You know me, through and through;*
> *my body is no mystery to You,*
> *or how I was secretly kneaded into shape*
> *and patterned in the depths of the Earth.*
> *You saw my limbs yet unformed in the womb*
> *and in Your records they were all recorded,*
> *day-by-day they were fashioned,*
> *not one limb was late in growing.*
> *How deep I find Your thoughtfulness, O my God!*
> *How inexhaustible are Your topics!*
> *Can I count them?*
> *They outnumber the grains of sand!*
> *To finish the count my years would have to equal Yours!*

Clearly, this psalmist is expressing an emotionally intense, personal relationship with the Eternal Source of every detail of our temporality. Not only our infant-hood, childhood, and adulthood, but also our life in the womb has been lived within the loving care for us by this Profound "Thou" of our personal God-devotion. Such personal intimacy with Yahweh reflects what Jeremiah was pointing to with a "new covenant written upon our hearts."

The prophets of the Old Testament breathed aliveness into a revolution in humanness that characterized those particular pre-Jesus centuries. Jesus was remembered as having to do with another "new covenant with Yahweh.:

Jeremiah by dealing deeply with his own time became for early Christians a predictor of Jesus. We do not have to believe in magical historical predictions to see Jeremiah as an archetype that Jesus also fulfilled—initiating a new covenant with Profound Reality.

Ezekiel
Resilience Amidst the Gloom

The story and teachings of Ezekiel are difficult to understand, for he says things in strange ways and he lives in a very complex and hard to fathom time in the destiny of the people of Yahweh. He and Jeremiah were both members of the priestly class in Judea at the time of the Babylonian exile, the conquest of Jerusalem, and the destruction of the Judean nation. Jeremiah was the older man and probably a mentor to Ezekiel. They were certainly colleagues and on the same side of facing up to these grim times and to seeing the delusions and unfaithfulness of the people of Judea at that time.

The exile to Babylon of Judean families took place in waves over a period of time. Ezekiel and his family went to Babylon in the first group of exiled people, while Jeremiah remained as the prophet of doom in Jerusalem until after the final dispersal of the nation including the the end of the reign of the puppet king appointed by the Babylonians. This arrogant and falsely optimistic king was unfaithful to both the Babylonians and to the Truth of a covenant loyalty to the Power of Profound Realty, affectionately named "Yahweh."

During the time between Ezekiel's exile and the complete fall of Judea, Ezekiel joined Jeremiah as a prophet of doom—calling into question the delusions of the Judean people left in Judea as well as the homesick Judean people who were with Ezekiel in exile. These delusions consisted of a false hope for a quick return to nationhood as well as a false perspective on the covenant righteousness of this people—the notion that being the people of Yahweh required a nation. Ezekiel painted this nation-clinging majority of Judean people as a harlot who instead of charging for her services bribed her clients to use her.

Both Jeremiah and Ezekiel saw their hope for a faithful Yahwist future within those who were carried off into exile. Jeremiah, after a time, went to Egypt with a group-that established a community of Jewish practice there, but he bought a piece of land in Judea as a witness of his hope for the return from Exile of those who then resided in Babylon.

Meanwhile, after the complete fall of Judea, Ezekiel changed the tone of his prophesy to one of outlandish hope. Most memorable among his strange metaphors was the story of the dry bones that took on flesh and awareness. He was referring to the hopeless despairing remnant of the people of Yahweh trapped in a foreign land, their mission of deep humanity to all the nations of the world apparently over—certainly over in the old form of being an invulnerable nation.

King Nebuchadnezzar, emperor of Babylon, got a harsh press in the various narratives of the Old Testament literature, but he was a merciful leader compared with many others. Instead of simply slaughtering the leadership of their conquests, they carried off the aristocracy and made use of them within Babylon's rather high class culture of those times. Nebuchadnezzar gave the Jewish exiles a life, and he let them practice their religion. Much was learned by the exiles from this powerful culture. The first chapter of the Bible was written using Babylonian science. The Biblical poetry reflects many gifts from Babylon culture, knowing this can help those of us who read Scripture today. The people who after their 49-year sojourn retuned home to Judea to rebuild a nation were a stronger people, as a whole, than those who were carried off. In case you don't believe me about King Nebuchadnezzar, following is a quote from Bernard Anderson's *Understanding the Old Testament:*

> *"Jews were given a good bit of social freedom and economic opportunity. . . . their lot in Babylon was a great deal better than that of modern Jews who have been crowded into dingy ghettos or herded into concentration camps. . . . Babylonian Jews were permitted to move about freely, to live in their communities in or near the great cities, and to carry on their way of life."*
>
> *"The most serious adjustment that the Jews of Babylon had to make was a religious adjustment. Their faith had been oriented to the land of Palestine, the inheritance that Yahweh had given them, the place that Yahweh had caused his name to dwell."[11]*

This new home was the context for Ezekiel's 20-year span of ministry in Babylon. He was a priest and he did priestly actions—liturgy, narratives, teaching, religious practices. He was a keeper of the heritage, a shaper of the narrative, and an inspiration to people who were embodying the Yahwist heritage. He was also a reformer of that heritage. It would have been easy for the whole community to assimilate into this strong culture of Babylon. Ezekiel and his allies were tough people relative to their faith. Many of them held to what was of most value in their deeply ancient heritage.

This toughness can seem strange or rigid of Ezekiel to be so true to his deep past. Ezekiel, however, was a wild man of religious forcefulness

---

[11] Andersson, Bernard, *Understanding the Old Testament*, Prentice Hall Inc. 1957, page 377

a story teller who made history, your history and mine.. If he had one outstanding teaching it was the Absolute Holiness of Yahweh. If we are among those who have any doubt about the living experience of that irrational Otherness of the Profound Reality of Yahweh, we would be scalded by Ezekiel's presence. We may have little idea about how much of Ezekiel characterizes our existing Bible. His people lived in exile in Babylon for 49 years before some of them came home to a broken-down Judea and built it anew.

Such a commitment to a Profound-Reality-honoring-religious practice has become rare in the contemporary Christian churches. Let Ezekiel have a place in your meditative counsel. He helped give an exiled people a sane passage through difficult times. He showed us the power of religious teachings and ritual for doing such a challenging feat.

SESSION EIGHT

Second Isaiah
Calling Us Home

The last chapters of the scroll of Isaiah (chapter 40 and following) contain writings of an unnamed prophet who lived in the closing days of the Babylonian Exile among the exiled Judean families whose exile began about 49 years earlier. The new historical situation of that time featured the conquests of the Babylonian Empire by the Persian Empire. The policies of this new leading force in history allowed exiles to return home to their native lands.

Many of these Judean families had become at home in Babylon and were opting to stay. Second Isaiah was rallying a band of Yahwist activists to go home to Judea and rebuild life for those now scattered and chaotic people. Without the success of this project, we might never have heard of the Mosaic breakthrough. This was being understood as a privilege to do this, but it was no easy task. Staying in Babylon was the easier choice.

Second Isaiah felt called to paint a very strong narrative about Yahweh as the God of history—featuring developments on this theme initiated by Amos, Hosea, First Isaiah, Jeremiah, and Ezekiel in recent years and in decades earlier. Here is some of Second Isaiah's powerful poetry.

> *Comfort, Comfort my people*
> *—it is the voice of your God*
> *Speak tenderly to Jerusalem*
> *and tell her this:*
> *That her penalty is paid:*
> *She has received from Yahweh's hand*
> *Double measure for all her sins.*

> *There is a voice that cries*
> *Prepare a Road for Yahweh through the wilderness,*
> *Clear a highway for our God.*
> *Every valley shall be lifted up*
> *Every mountain and hill bright down*
> *And mountain ranges become a plain*
> *Thus shall the glory of Yahweh be revealed*
> *And all humankind together shall see it.*
> *For Yahweh himself has spoken.*

> *A voice says, "Cry",*
> *And another asks, "What shall I cry?"*
> *That all humankind is grass. [including Babylon and Judea]*
> *They last no longer than a flower of the field.*

The grass withers, the flower fades,
When the breath of Yahweh blows upon them.
The grass withers, the flowers fade,
but the word of our God endures for evermore.
Isaiah40:1-8

And here is a passage that is more specific:

Thus says Yahweh, your ransomer,
Who fashioned you from birth.
I, Yahweh, who made all things
By myself I stretched out the skies.
Alone, I hammered out the floor of the Earth.
I frustrate false prophets and their signs,
And make fools of diviners
I reverse what wise men say
And make nonsense of their wisdom
I make my servants' prophecies come true.
And give effect to my messengers designs.
I say to Jerusalem,
"She shall be inhabited once more,"
And of the cities of Judah, they shall be rebuilt.
All their ruins I will restore.
I say to the deep water [to Babylon] "Be dried up;
I say to Cyrus, "You shall be my shepherd.
To carry out my purpose.
So that Jerusalem may be rebuilt.
And the foundations of the temple may be laid.
Isaiah: 44:24-28

Second Isaiah saw Cyrus, the Emperor of Persia, as the servant of

Yahweh opening the way for and issuing the calling to these Yahwists in Babylon exile for their return to Judea after their families had been in exile in Babylon, some of them, for the last 49 years.

This was seen as Yahweh calling for some hard travel to do some very hard work. They saw these sacrifices in the context of obedience to the God of Abraham, Isaac, and Jacob as well as Moses, Joshua and so on. Jesus, in the poetry of John, is supposed to have said, "My Father is working and I am working." Second Isaiah might be said to have pre-staged this Johanine spirit—a spirit about what we might call "attuned working" with Profound Reality.

"Attuned working" for us in the time of Putin, Trump, and other authoritarian demolishers of democracy is also a calling to hard work that we members of these 21ˢᵗ century societies can recognize. In this 21ˢᵗ century, we can also notice the Yahwist calling to "attuned working" being issued to and being taking in by people who do not practice, Jewish, Christian, or Islamic religion. One of the revelatory happenings to us today is that we are called to live in an inter-religious era. We are speaking of and to the same spirit realities with different religious languages—languages as different from the West as Buddhism, Hinduism and Taoism. May strong Christian voices continue to bring the poetry of Second Isaiah to the tables of religious dialogue going on today.

Let us listen together to Second Isaiah calling us "homeward" to the revelations that have activated the long histories of our various religions traditions and to the opening in our current cultures for some much improved vision on acting humanly realistic.

And let us give fresh restatement to the power narratives that previous prophets have powered the actions of those previous applications of our various revelatory gifts and to the applications called for today by our also troubled times.

C. THE NEW TESTAMENT STORIES

A 6-session introductory course

SESSION ONE

THE NEW TESTIMONY OF STORIES are built upon the Old testimony of stories that are built upon the viewpoint of the Exodus revelation. "Old" here does not mean out of date, or lesser than, but rather foundational for the "New." In other words, the "New" testimony means a new viewpoint upon the "Old" testimony. but not a rejection of the Old testimony.

This newness also means a new set of religions practices that include the baptism washing from our evil eras, and the bread and wine meal of a new covenant with the same Profound Reality called "God" or "Jahweh"—later "Lord" and "Allah. This One Profound Reality, that is present within all realities, unites Judaism, Christianity, and Islam in a grand sisterhood of Arabian originated religions of various forms of radical monotheism.

It is a very important part of he New Testament stories that the Old Testament texts remain relevant even though they are seen anew through the "eyes" of the New Testament viewpoint. It is also important to say that the Old viewpoint remains an important check upon the New viewpoint as well as important support for it. Judaism and Christianity remain very close sister religious practices with much more in common than for their also important differences. Those differences are mostly about basic rituals and pageants with an also differing accompanying style of theologizing. Though this New Testament theological discussions of our relations with Profound Reality are different in some basic metaphorical theological content from the Old Testament theologizing, the Profound Reality of the New Testament is the same Profound Reality as the Old Testament. The Hebrew Bible is not old for the Jewish set of religions. And the Old Testament is still scripture for the Christian set of religions. The Christian New Testament is a fresh viewpoint that makes the Old Testament New. This understanding will be further elaborated in much more detail in the following examples.

Let me explain the error of a so-called "post-theology" Christian movement, using the deconstruction movement in philosophy. Deconstruction can only deconstruct what has been constructed by the rational constructions of human thoughtfulness. The God metaphor that is referenced in both Old and New Testament theologizing is the One Profound Reality—an ontological or being reference that cannot be deconstructed. All our philosophies and theologies are humanly constructed and can, therefore, be deconstructed, but a revelation of Almighty God cannot be deconstructed, for this "revelation" is not a rational breakthrough, but a real experience that includes the finitude of all human reasoning and thoughtfulness when confronting this incomprehensible Profound Reality we cannot fully escape. Revelation takes us out of our minds and then brings us back to the great gifts of our minds to think about this sort of vision quest type of inward journey with huge outward consequences.

Furthermore, the New Testament revelation is not about an eighth Chakra as postulated by some mystics. The New Testament revelation is Profound Reality experience that takes place *in this world*, not as an invasion from a separate world. There is no such thing as an eight chakra in Buddhism or Hinduism or any other valid religion. Chakra 7 is human consciousness raised to its "speed-of light-limit," so to speak. There is no faster spin of profound consciousness than chakra 7 as approximately described in Part 1 A. Chakra 7 is top speed, so to speak, no matter what religious practice is being practiced to access this profound consciousness of Profound Realty. A chakra 8 advocate is actually undoing the entire chakra model in order to advocate a misleading self affirmation.

We might think of religious practice as an eighth topic (not a more intense consciousness). For example, if the first three Noble Truths of Buddhism are about the profound consciousness of Profound Reality, then the fourth Noble Truth is about religious practices—an eightfold path of practices that can open access to that profound consciousness of Profound Reality. Similarly the stories of the Christian Bible are paths of religious practice that make the enlightenment of profound consciousness of Profound Reality more likely to human beings. Buddhism and Christianity, in spite of their vast differences in practice, are practices for accessing the same profound consciousness of Profound Reality and for learning how to live our lives from that deep place of a profound rest, joy, bliss, and responsibility.

The New testimony stories center on Jesus, a completely ordinary human, understood as Messiah or Christ, yet these stories can only be properly understood if their Old Testament stories are remembered. Some of these writers claim that this Christ revelation is a New Exodus that does not in any way dismiss the first Exodus, but is a new convent with the same God, somewhat like what Jeremiah created of a "new convent of the heart" for the survival of the Mosaic heritage under the conditions of its exile in Babylon.

The notion that the Old Testament is about wrath and the New Testament is about love is a Christian heresy of the most severe mis-understandings of both wrath and love. To put part of this misunderstanding in one sentence. "The wrath of God is itself love for humans, for this so-called wrath is Profound Reality's enduring "Realism" that is indeed a wrath of opposition to our many human-made substitutions for Reality, fashioned by our busy minds and rebelling wills. It is these humanly originating substitute "realities" for Profound Reality that is the root "origin" of the wrath of God. Like all such theological sentences it takes whole books to spell out the implications of such a Biblical direction for our thoughtfulness.

In the following New Testament story interpretations, I will be attempting to illustrate how these much ignored or much misunderstood bits of Christian scripture can be "resurrected" for our times as "true-to Reality." For example, "Gospel" means a *"proclamation"* of good news to the whole world and to every human in it. Finally, "Gospel" means a *"call for my or your choice"* to join in a continuing "crisis-of-decisions" that redirects our whole lives from our deep unrealisms into our still deeper realisms. Christianity, like Judaism and Islam, is an activist religion. We deepen our journey in Christian faithfulness by *doing* the faith—teaching, serving, contemplating, and structurally changing society in its rules and practices of justice. I will speak more to this later, but let us note, for now, that Christians who know their faith do not tolerate any authoritarian power addict, especially one who wants to escape from all accountability, from taking leadership in any justice-building process. Those who want to confuse Christian faith with fascism are misunderstanding both.

The Good News Proclamations

Let us begin by noting that the New Testament collection of stories begins with the Matthew, Mark, Luke, and John works that call themselves "Gospels"—namely, a Good News that can be proclaimed to the entire world.

Mark was the first of these four Gospels to be written in about 65-70 CE—almost four decades beyond the crucifixion. Mark was written to be read aloud to small communities of people that Paul and his other companions had organized among Old Testament Scripture readers and hearers. We might say that Mark invented the Gospel as a mode of literature that did not exist in this quality of excellence before Mark penned this first Gospel of the New Testament.

Matthew was written later using most of the content of the Mark beginning with this new literacy innovation and added more content, especially remembered teaching of Jesus. Matthew was written for a wider circle of Jewish-practicing people. Matthew had a different style of theologizing than Mark. Matthew sees Jesus as a new rabbi with new teachings, while in Mark we see the meaning of Jesus as a secret that Mark is tricking the readers into hearing with the ears of our contemplative selves. In Mark's literary devise, three women bringing spices to the Jesus tomb are the first to learn the secret of resurrected humanity. These women found resurrection dreadful because they saw it was they themselves who were to bear this dreadful resurrection—themselves becoming the body of Christ. They left the tomb, but in terror saying nothing at first.

Luke meanwhile was adding still other content to Mark and was directing his version of the Good News to the more Gentile wing of the expanding Christ-way Jewish practice. Luke sees Jesus as a leader of leaders for a whole new humanity. Luke writes a second book *The Acts of the Apostles*, making clear that the resurrected body of Christ was present in Peter, in Paul and in a host of Marys, James-es, and others.

It was in Mark's writings that we first see the notion that the new spirit wine of the Gospel Good News that Peter and Paul were stirring up in their Christ-way Judaism was now requiring a whole new wineskin of religious practice. This new wineskin can be viewed as a call for a new religion, a new religious practice that came to be called "Christianity." This leads us into the realization that Christianity is a religious practice alongside other religious practices, and that the Profound Realty that Christians worship as their God is not owned by the Christian churches. Profound Reality is there for everyone whatever their religious practice or their lack of one. The Good News is human news not news for Christian only. And Christians do not possess the Good News as a doctrine they can hold in their ego-serving minds. They serve whole humans, not just minds, with a new awareness of their deep consciousness. The Good News witness is himself or herself grasped by that Good News that they are then called to share with others—indeed, proclaim to everyone.

Jesus was a Jew, lived as a Jew, died as a Jew. His contribution was a new Judaism, not a new religion. Peter, and the other first disciple leaders or apostles were likewise still Jews in their religious practices. Paul's letter writings made some big changes in the meaning of "law," and Paul's letters were later selected for the New Testament collection of books; nevertheless, Paul and his first circles of people can be viewed as Christ-way Jews rather than as Christian practitioners. I am going to consistently claim that in Paul's thinking in the 50s CE, we find that the new religion of Christianity did not yet exist. I am further suggesting that Mark's remarkable work was a call to practice a new religion (Christianity) that was breaking loose from its Jewish framework of thoughtfulness and pageants.

Even so, Mark. Mathew. and Luke, all three, are deeply embedded in the Hebrew Bible's Greek translation. Their writings might be called historical fiction. They were certainly not scientific biographies of Jesus. They were three types of theologizing that were very much alike in their emphasis on cross and resurrection. We have called them the Synoptic Gospels. I repeat, these books lead the collection we call "the New Testament."

The Gospel of John was still a Gospel—a proclamation of the same Good News—but it was not even close to a plausible historical fiction. It was more like a stage play. Following is how we might imagine it being performed on a stage:

Before the curtain opens a very old man in a wheel chair roles out in front to the curtain and faces the audience. He stares at them for a moment; then he proclaims in a very loud voice: "When all things began this Proclamation of Good News already was. Not one thing was created without this Good News being present in it."

He then wheels off as the curtain rises and we see a line of people being baptized in the river Jordan. Dressed in rough attire, the ritual leader has a placard on his chest, "The Baptizer." The old man from the off-stage wings says loudly "Being washed of an evil era." In this line of people to be baptized is a man wearing a placard that reads "Son of a roof repair man from Nazareth." From the wings these same words are also said loudly as Jesus undergoes the dunking. After he is baptized the placard on Jesus's chests reads "Light of the World." The whole stage turns dark except for a light on this individual and his placard. From the wings, the old man voice concludes this scene with these loudly spoken words: "The light shines in the darkness and the darkness has not overcome it."

The curtains closes and then reopens on the scene of a big festival or party. A woman bears the placard "His mother." She is talking with "Light of the World" about the lack of wine at this party. "Light of the World" orders tall vessels to be filled with water. "Light of the world" blesses the water and when people drink it they are all smiling. One of them comes to the front of the stage and proclaims to the audience "The host of this party, instead of serving the good wine first and saving the inferior wine for last, has saved the best wine till last". The curtain closes.

When the curtain opens, the old-man voice from off stage says: "A Pharisee named Nicodemus, a member of the Jewish Council, came by night to see Jesus, the "Light of the World." We see these two individuals on a moderately darkened stage having the conversation that is laid out in John 3:1-21.

The whole Gospel of John can be viewed in this rather outlandish manner of envisioning the stage-like nature of this truly alternative sort of writing. The Gospel of John is much more elaborated then my brief sketch, but perhaps the above paraphrase makes my point that the nature of this piece of literature is something very different from the Synoptic Gospels. It is more like a stage play than a plausible narrative of fiction.

Symbolic stories created by this innovative theologian is what we are reading in this Fourth Gospel. To me, the freedom of this writer to push the edges of Gospel writing this far is awesome. Also awesome to me is the freedom of the New Testament selection committees who allowed this piece of writing to be included in their scriptures. This entire early community of faith requires of us, in this religiously confused 21st century, to take a much closer look at these religious origins.

SESSION TWO

Jesus and the Kingdom of God

Since the Gospels are not biographies of Jesus, what evidence for a biography of Jesus do we have. Scholars have found a way to see within the writings of these first three Gospels some approximate scientific glimpses of the earliest layers in the formation of these Gospels. The very earliest layer is still just memories of the earliest disciples, but we can derive a better glimpses to the Jesus of Nazareth figure using these careful studies. Rudolf Bultmann's book *Jesus and the Word* is a classic attempt to understand for our century these earliest scraps of the Jesus heritage. We see here a picture of a Jesus who is a loyal Jew, loyal to the Almighty Jahweh, a believer in the resurrection of the body at the end of time when Jahweh judges all our lives.

We can also see today, with our existential eyes, that this end-of-time myth, though strange to our science-trained ears, is only a story—a myth, a fiction that means for us personally that none of us are getting away with our commitments to unrealism, and that Reality wins in the end, that God rules, and that God's humanity will be restored to its created shape in the end. The coming Christ was understood as the final human come from the end of time.

Jesus' preaching on the Kingdom of God is about this end-of-time judgement happening now in the lives of those listening to Jesus' roadside and hillside proclamations. Right now, Jesus is saying, we are experiencing the end of time—the conclusion of Satin's rule over our humanity and a restoration of our essential (or created) humanity. Jesus's Kingdom of God is often seen as an Eternal place that we go after we die, but this is not what Jesus meant. The Kingdom is coming now on this Earth among this fallen humanity. "Thy kingdom come on Earth, as it is in the essence of things."

Also the Kingdom of God is a sociological image; it speaks of a community of people into whom individuals are being born, rather than a merely psychological image in the secrecy of individual psyches. This community is also a sort of secret society in the sense that we never know for sure who are the members of it or what are the social boundaries of it. But this presence is real in history, in humanity, in action. "The sociological metaphor of the "Resurrected Body-of-Christ" is another metaphor for the "Kingdom of God" taught by Jesus. "The Body of Christ" became more used than the "Kingdom of God" after the "in Christ" theologizing of Paul. Both metaphors are about a living community of people within human history rather than a place to go after our temporal historicity is over,.

Though not synonymous with any Christian denomination, "The Body Christ" may, nevertheless, be present in some of these institutions as it also is in some communities that are not practicing a Christian religion. Joining a church is not the same thing as becoming a member of the Body of Christ. Being a practicing member of a Christian community can make this "new birth" to "the Kingdom of God" or " the Body of Christ" more likely.

And this Body of Christ (Kingdom of God) does build on Earth manifestations of deep aliveness, deep community, and deep justice for all humans as well as care for all the other life forms. Justice is conceived and built by human beings, not dropped down from heaven. This kingdom of God is human beings building new community and new justice on Earth for everyone. "Dear Jahweh, Thy Kingdom come on Earth as it is the essence of things."

For Jesus, this Kingdom of God as an antithesis to the Kingdom of Rome. We lovers of democracy can glean from these sayings of Jesus to his disciples that this "Kingdom of God" is very different from the "Kingdom of Rome," more different than democracy is from authoritarianism. Here is a quote from Mark 10:42-44, with my bits of up-dating:

> *You know that the so-called rulers of the heathen world lord it over* [everyone], *and their great men have absolute power. But it must not be so among you. No, whoever*

among you wants to be great must become the servant of you all, and if he (or she) wants to be first among you, he (or she) must be [in servitude] *to all* [humans]*!*

Peter and his Pentecostal Sermon

Pentecost might be remembered as a memorial to the crucified Jesus for the thousands of people who had been in some way touched by the life and death of Jesus. The Awe experienced by the people at this gathering seemed to settle on the heads of those in attendance like flames of fire. This so-called fire was a whole group event, noticeable by those in attendance who had eyes to see the Awe shining forth from the Awesome, Almighty, Profound Reality into the faces and attitudes of almost every one there.

Peter rose to interpret what was happening. He said something rather surprising for both then and now. He said this fiery Awe meant that Jesus had risen from the dead to be the expected Christ, come from the end of time—indicating that those assembled were the "body of the Christ" expected at the end of time. Peter (or perhaps his followers) further spelled out that the imperative of this happening was to go forth to all the world a tell this Good News to all who would hear it. Peter's bit of strange metaphorical thoughtfulness was given by a mere bold, working-man fisherman. Nevertheless, Peter pulled together some high-energy and then well-known metaphors into a vision for a new birth of realism in human living. Being the resurrected body of Christ meant something to Peter. It can mean something to us as well.

SESSION THREE

Paul and Theological Letter Writing

Paul has been both severely misunderstood and mistakenly opposed because he was not understood. I am going to try to reveal the true Paul with two bits of his theologizing using a method I am calling "solving for the unknown."

Romans 1 – Everybody Knows X

Let us look carefully at what Paul means when he used the word "God." The following passage from Paul's letter to the Romans will do. I will use the "X" substitution method to bypass the ideas that our minds typically attach to the word "God." Then, we will be able to solve this portion of Paul's letter for the meaning of the word "God" to Paul and to those who heard him speak this word. (I am using J.B. Phillips translation of Romans 1:18-24 and for clarity, and I am again adding a few parenthetical phrases.)

> *Now the holy anger* [awesome fury] *of X is disclosed from Heaven* [the realm of Mystery] *against the godlessness and evil of those persons who render truth dumb and inoperative by their wickedness. It is not that they do not know the truth about X; indeed X has made it quite plain to them. For since the beginning of the world the invisible attributes of X, e.g. X's eternal power and divinity, have been plainly discernible through things which X has made and which are commonly seen and known, thus leaving these persons without a rag of excuse. They knew all the time that there is X, yet they refused to acknowledge X*

as such, or to thank X for what X is and does. Thus they
became fatuous in their argumentations, and plunged their
silly minds still further into the dark. Behind a façade of
"wisdom" they became just fools, fools who would exchange
the glory [awesomeness] *of the immortal X for an imitation*
image of a mortal human, or of creatures that run or fly or
crawl. They gave up X: and therefore X gave them up to be
the playthings of their own foul desires ....

So, what content for X does Paul's text assume? If we fill in what we noted in Session 2 as a meaning for X in Psalm 90, this Pauline text is also well illuminated. If we assume that God is an idea in a human head that makes sense of everything (or at least many things), we can see that such a substitution does not fit the text. Indeed, any idea of God that humans create illustrates what Paul is pointing to with his phrase "an imitation image of a mortal human." Any image, model, or art piece that humans have created is not X. X is not created by humans. X is what creates (posits in being) stars, rocks, plants, animals and all their creations and humans and all their creations.

Why can Paul say that humans already know X? This is so because what Paul means by X is the boundless power that is "discernible" in all the things that are commonly seen and known. Paul also claims that something called the "divinity" of X is "discernible" in all the things that are commonly seen and known. By "divinity" he probably means some sort of glory, majesty, or awesomeness that goes with the enormous power already mentioned. X is "invisible" but the effects of X are not invisible. Everything that has the power of being is empowered by X. Humans cannot get their minds around X, but their "deep inner beings" discern the presence of X. Clearly, X is the Awesome Mysteriousness that is creating, supporting, and ending every visible thing. The failure of humanity is not a lack of experience of X, but the refusal to come to terms with X and to worship X as their life meaning. Such worship means nothing more nor less than being realistic, for X is Reality with a capital R. Such capitalization is symbolic of boundless and inescapable power not created by human hands. X is not "a reality" created by humans to fit their preferences. X is the Reality that undermines every fragment of false reality created by humans. X is the Infinite Truth that judges all our finite efforts toward truthfulness as well as all our overt lies.

Paul uses the word "Heaven." This is a key word in Paul's metaphorical system of thinking about profound experience. In fact it is a key word for Jesus and all the other teachers and authors in the entire biblical collection. But "heaven" is not part of our metaphorical vocabulary today. "Heaven" has died as a useful metaphor. We now know that there is no transcendent space in a literal sense – no angels, no devils, no gods and goddesses, no Big Person up there to take care of us. We no longer live in a double-deck universe. Furthermore, we can no longer helpfully use the double-deck metaphor as a metaphor for talking about Ultimate Reality. We need to use other metaphors, and millions of us already do so. We can describe these deep experiences of our lives, and we often use non-two-story means to share our experiences of that Enigmatic Awesomeness—an Overall Profound Reality that is streaming through our experience of ordinary objects, events, and persons.

Most of us today have great difficulty understanding how those who lived in the pre-modern past eras could talk about their primal experiences using the double-deck mode of talking. Most people think that those ancestors took supernatural space literally, as contemporary fundamentalists attempt to do. But the ancients were not taken up with our modern categories of "literal" and "non-literal." They lived quite comfortably in their double-deck universe of poetic imagery. There was ordinary space and there was "divine" space. They may or may not have noticed that this double-deck picture was merely a metaphor created by the human mind. In any case, the metaphor served them well as a way to talk about the profound matters of their existence.

It may be hard for contemporary people to grasp that Luther, Thomas Aquinas, and Augustine were not literalists, but "existentialists" who knew (in their own way) that the double-deck metaphor was a metaphor. Jesus was also this kind of existentialist. When Jesus prayed "Our Father who art in heaven" he was saying to his culture what it would mean for us to say in our culture, "Like a good parent to us are You, Oh Awesome Mysteriousness shining through every rock, hair, and leaf of nature." The great saints of the past were not dumber than us: they simply used a different metaphorical language.

When we clearly understand this shift in metaphorical language, we can translate Paul's text into twenty-first century talk without losing what Paul was pointing to in his own life and without requiring ourselves to pretend that we can use his metaphorical language. With our own language we can point in our own lives to the very same dynamics of existence that Paul was sharing with us.

Today, as well as then, everybody knows X, the same X that Paul was talking about. But few of us acknowledge X and worship X as the core meaning of our lives. Also, it is still true that the masses of our age have given up X and therefore X has given them up to be the playthings of their own foul desires. "Foul desires" covers more than our drug addictions or our sex addictions. Foul desires means our discomfort with another genders than our own. Our core foulness has to do with our desire to be the creator of our own reality, rather than allowing our true lives be given to us by X.

So what is X? X is the Reality for which we are making a substitution when we create our own reality. Birds do not try to create their own reality. Squirrels do not try to create their own reality. They perceive and interpret their experience with mental products we might call multi-sensory reruns. They do not use the type of mental products we call symbols. For example, four is a symbol used by humans to see a common quality between four clouds, four days, and four dogs. Among living species only humans have such a capacity. Humans (using the symbols of mathematics, language, art, and religious forms) have the capacity to put together a mental picture that can be substituted for Reality. Our ability to do this is a great and useful gift, but it also presents us with a temptation not faced by birds and squirrels. The temptation is to live in terms of the pictures we have created rather than the Reality we are attempting to picture. Our yielding to this temptation makes us the most dangerous species on the planet. Our yielding to this temptation means that we worship our own creations, a state of living that Paul interprets as rebellion against Reality, the Reality for which we have built a substitute reality. While it may seem almost inevitable that humans confuse their own pictures of reality with Reality, Paul is saying that there is no excuse for it.

Furthermore, Reality "responds" to our unrealistic substitutions with the consequences that derive from our trusting in those substitutes. We don't get rid of Reality or the Power of Reality by building our substitutes. Since we have given up Reality for substitutions, Reality gives us up to the consequences of our living with substitutes. Paul sees this substitution process as the primal root of the corruption of the human species. And he calls it "foolishness." Let us hear Paul's words again:

> *Behind a façade of "wisdom" they became just fools, fools who would exchange the glory* [awesomeness] *of the immortal X for an imitation image of a mortal human, or of creatures that run or fly or crawl. They gave up X: and*

therefore X gave them up to be the playthings of their own
foul desires ....

So when we see humanity waging wars in defense of their religious creations, we are seeing humanity in the state of having been given up by X to be the playthings of their own foul desires. When we see humanity abusing and belittling persons who do not fit into their cult-group of beliefs and morals, we are seeing humanity in the state of having been given up by X to be the playthings of their own foul desires. When we see humanity destroying the planet in the name of free enterprise, economic growth, a still bigger population of humans, a style of wastefulness, a consumer obsession, or any other substitute for sober realism, we are seeing humanity in the state of having been given up by X to be the playthings of their own foul desires. When we see humanity killing the truth tellers of their times rather than listening to them and changing their ways, we are seeing humanity in the state of having been given up by X to be the playthings of their own foul desires.

In other words, this is the core problem—humanity: having given up Reality for a substitute. Our being stuck within the substitutes that we have created to replace Reality is the consequence that Paul describes as Reality having given us up to be the plaything of our substitute unrealisms. And, according to Paul, there is no excuse for this. Here are Paul's words on excuses:

> *It is not that they do not know the truth about X;*
> *indeed X has made it quite plain to them. For since*
> *the beginning of the world the invisible attributes of X,*
> *e.g. X's eternal power and divinity, have been plainly*
> *discernible through things which X has made and which*
> *are commonly seen and known, thus leaving these persons*
> *without a rag of excuse.*

Reality is mysterious to the finite human mind, yet our elemental conscious being can experience this Mysteriousness. Because of this Absolutely Mysterious, Reality is beyond our mental reach, yet this Mysteriousness is discernible in the depths of human awareness and freedom. X is commonly seen and known. Mysterious Reality is not some far away idea that we have not yet grasped. Mysterious Reality is like a truck crashing into the side of our car. Mysterious Reality reaches us through some snake biting our toe, some cancer growing in our bowels. Mysterious Reality reaches us through a large host of pleasant things as well. Reality touches us in the "miracle" of having been born at all. Reality comes to us through the gift of our amazing body and its intricate functioning. Reality is the entire Mystery of all these Reality empowered "actualities" that we cannot avoid. There is no excuse for making substitutes for Reality and then (1) forgetting that they are substitutes and thereby entering into the illusion that these substitutes are Reality or (2) using these substitutes as our base for fighting against Reality.

By "fighting against Reality" we mean viewing Reality as our enemy because Reality does not operate by our values. Violent destruction is as much a part of Reality as surprising creation. A mega-star violently explodes. A volcano, flood, storm, or fire destroys a whole town or city. A cheetah runs down an antelope and eats it. A band of humans slaughter another band of humans. People often protest that any Reality that empowers or permits such violence cannot be "good" enough (by our standards) to deserve our worship. So we create some other "being" to be our "good," our "God," our "worship." Perhaps we imagine that this self-created "being" is real enough and powerful enough to interfere with the course of nature on our behalf. Paul wants us to know that these gods of our own creation do not even exist. Yet our devotion to them, turns our life to foulness.

There is no divine being coming to rescue us from Reality. And our fight with Reality is far worse than useless. Reality always wins. Fighting against Reality is a hopeless way to live. As Søren Kierkegaard so intricately describes, fighting Reality results in despair. There are many forms of despair: unconscious despair; painfully conscious secret despair; suicide, restless plunging into sensuality or noble work;; defiantly creating and defending a fake self; defiantly becoming a living proof to our selves that Reality is no damned good. All of these states of despair are needless; and the alternative is close at hand – namely, humbling ourselves before Reality in trust that the Reality that is actually confronting us is providing for us the best case scenario for our lives. According to Paul this is the "faith" that saves us from the despair (hell) we have been cast into because we have worshiped our creations rather than that Final Creative Force from which we cannot escape.

So what is "God" in the texts of Paul? It is that Mysterious, Awesome, Unrelenting, Inescapable Reality that has posited us, sustains us, and will inevitably eliminate us from the course of history. This X, this God, is a daily confrontation that everyone knows who is willing to know what they know. Is this "knowing" a belief in some alien Big Other that takes away our freedom and responsibility? No, X is not a belief at all. It is a conscious noticing. We can simply notice that the Reality that is actually confronting us is positing us in being with our freedom and responsibility. Our primal act of freedom is choosing to be free rather than vegetating in all our excuses and withdrawals and compulsions. Our primal act of freedom is choosing whether or not we will serve and obey the Reality that is limiting us as well as providing us with our freedom and our options (possibilities) toward the future.

The inexcusable "sin" of which Paul is accusing us is our rebellion against the actual limits and possibilities of our lives in favor of some substitute, some unreality that we have created to match our preferences for a life that is different from the one that we cannot escape. This self-created attitude results in bondage, not freedom. When we are in our freedom, we are free to rebel against Reality, but this rebellion creates bondage. When we use our freedom to rebel against Reality, our freedom is spent: we are thus delivered up to unfreedom, to bondage, to being the plaything of our own foul desires.

As strange as this may sound, a devotion to the Final Determining Power liberates us to be our full freedom—our being Profound-Reality "determined" does not mean that we are a tale already told, just waiting to unfold. No, our freedom will create part of the tale. The Determining Power is determining us to be freedom. When we rebel against this Power we create for ourselves some sort of box in which we live, separated from Reality and from the reality of our freedom. And this box is an alive state of living, a compulsive, defensive, destructive slavery from which we will have to be rescued or we will end up in the hell of despair.

The above New Testament revelations are clarifying further by this passage from the Gospel of Mark, a book I will discuss more later. Here is Mark 12:28-31 from Philips translation:

> *The one of the scribes approached him. He had been listening to that discussion and noticing how well Jesus had answered them, and he put this questions to him* [to Jesus].
> *"What are we to consider the greatest command of all."*
> *"The first and most important one is this," Jesus replied. "Here O Israel: 'the Lord our God, the Lord is one: and thou shall love the Lord* [Jahweh] *as Thy God with all thy heart and with all thy soul* [profound consciousness], *and with all thy mind, and with all thy strength.' The second is this, 'Thou shall love thy neighbor as thy self.' No other commandment is greater than these."*

The first of these two commandments is a summary of the first five commandments in Exodus 20. The second of these commandments is a summary of the last five commandments of Exodus 20. Jesus' second commandment means that we treat our self as one of our neighbors that we love. In other words we love all our neighboring realities being given to us by that Profound Reality that meets us in every neighbor including our own body and conscious life.

This means that Jesus' second commandment is like unto the first in the sense that love of Profound Reality is an ongoing journey of detachment form the human ego and therefore to the freedom to see our neighbors as equal to our love of self.

Some may complain that this "God" of Paul's is not personal. This is not true. It is very personal for Paul. It is his devotion, his papa/mama, his cause, his drive, his life, his personal worship even unto death. The vision of a big Person in some parallel universe that assists us to rebel against Paul's X is sheer illusion. No such Big Person exists. In that sense Paul is an atheist. He does not trust in the gods that humans create. He only trusts the UNCREATED CREATOR of his and our whole lives.

SESSION FOUR

More of Paul's words: "God is in Christ reconciling the world to Himself."

With this next verse from Paul's letters, I will expand my mathematical trick to two more unknowns—"Y" and "W": **X is in Y reconciling W to X.**

What does it mean for "God to be in Christ reconciling the world to Himself." (2nd Corinthians 5: 19) This saying of Paul's has been much preached upon, but clarity about the meaning of this formula has been much confused. Let us assume that we have begun to solve for X in the Romans passage above. What Paul means by "God" or "X" is an experience of Eternal Mystery, the incomprehensible Source of all things, the eternal power and divinity that have been plainly discernible through things which "X has made and which are commonly seen and known."

In this second passage, Paul is saying that X, this Eternal Mystery, was in Christ reconciling *the world* to X, the Eternal Mystery. Paul does not say that the Eternal Mystery became Jesus, a historical figure. It is superstition to say that incarnation means that the Eternal became the man Jesus. The incarnation means something else. Jesus was God in the sense that the Eternal became Present in this flesh and blood person, Jesus, in a way that was healing to humanity. If we do not understand what it means for one of us to be the place where the Eternal becomes Present in a way that is healing to humanity, then we do not understand how this was true for Jesus.

Here is a crass illustration of the possible connection of our capacities with those of Jesus. Imagine me a 22-year-old seminary student pastoring my first church. I am standing in the pulpit of that small church sharing a simplified sermon from Paul Tillich's. *The Shacking of the Foundations*. Half of the congregation finds this enlivening. The other half are seeking to get me replaced. Consider the proposition that Gene Marshall is the place where the Eternal becomes Present in a way that is healing to humanity. Whether that was so, we cannot be sure. But that being so is what we mean by seeing God being present in Jesus. This is a paradox that actually happens in history, that we cannot with our fragile minds fully own or control.

When Jesus dies upon the cross, this is not the dying of the Eternal Mystery. This is not that death of what the Apostles Creed is referring to with the term "Almighty God." "Almighty God" means the Eternal Mystery which does not die. The cross is the outpouring of the life of Jesus in obedience to the Almighty aspect of the three-faced experience we call "The Trinity"—The Almighty, the Jesus revelation, and the Holy Spirit. Consider Jesus, as he is pictured in the story of the Garden of Gethsemane. Jesus is facing his torture to death the next day. He says. "Not my will, but thy will be done." Jesus is not the enteral dying of God. Jesus is a mere human being in whom the Everlasting Eternal Mystery is present to awakening humanity and whose life and witness is being rejected by a fallen humanity.

So what does it mean for X (the Almighty) to be in Y (Christ) reconciling W (the fallen world) to X (the Almighty)? What does Paul mean by Y (by "Christ"), in this text? It is clear that Paul associates the man Jesus with the title Christ, but "Christ" has a wider meaning than we commonly see when Paul says that the community of those who accept Jesus as the Christ are "in Christ." Further, to be "in Christ" means that we share in the crucifixion and in the resurrection. How is that so? What is crucified and what is resurrected?

We can begin by saying that our crucifixion means that our expectations for a Messiah who would save us from the terrors of Almighty God was very rudely killed. Jesus was and still is a disappointment in terms of being a Messiah who would rescue us from the tyranny of the Roman Empire, or from the British Empire, or from the U.S. Empire, or from a racist society, or from our civilization's momentum toward ecological doom. In terms of such expectations, Jesus was and is a failed Messiah. His death (as well as his life and teachings) killed our expectations for the arrival of someone (or some event) that would rescue us from the grim and grimy tasks of resolving our own earthly affairs of spirit health and social justice.

Furthermore, those among us who have given up our expectation for a false messiah are going to be swimming upstream, for the fallen world is taken up with false expectations of many sorts. Here are some: When I get a new job, then I will be really living. When I find a proper mate, then I will be really living. When my children finally leave home, then I will have life at last. When my health returns to normal then -----. When some pill my doctor gives me, dissolves my most troubling pains, then ----. There is no such Messiah on the way. And for Jesus to be your Messiah means you have renounced all such messianic expectations. With a Jesus sort of Messiah—that is, a "Jesus Christ," there is just our living now with its possibilities and responsibilities. There is just you and I who, like Jesus, face the challenging demands of the Almighty God to expend our lives for something worth expending it for, and to do so before our life simply expends itself. Jesus in his teachings again and again explained that clinging on to whatever we cling to what has been, or is hoped for, will mean the loss our true life. We who are "in Christ" move from clinging to flinging. We who are "in Christ" are flung and are flinging ourselves into experiencing a resurrection of the Life that was in Christ Jesus. And this Life takes place, not tomorrow, nor yesterday, but Now.

So being "in Christ" means flinging our life into the Now of our own times. This means flinging ourselves into the climate crisis or into whatever else calls us in our moment of living on this Earth. For Jesus it meant questioning the moralistic use in his time of an oppressive understanding of the Mosaic Law. Jesus called people to simply fling themselves into a forgiveness that was universally present. Forgiveness is not stopped by how messy our past lives have been. Now the kingdom of God was being offered to us as our true home – the entry into which means flinging ourselves into an ever-forgiving new start that is present in each and every living Now in which we are being posited by the

Ever-Present, Eternal, Almighty, Mysteriousness. Such flinging of our lives "in Christ" is the core meaning of experiencing the resurrection.

It may be helpful to recall that Paul was a Jew who knew what the old myths meant when they said that the Messiah was the essential human scheduled for the end of time when all estrangement from our essential humanity would be exposed, judged, and destroyed. In other words when the Almighty restores humanity to its essence. The Good News proclamation of Peter and Paul was the announcement that this judgement and this restoration was happening now in the work of Jesus. The meaning of "resurrection" was simply that those of us being healed by the Jesus Christ happening were being reborn into the body of Christ—that is, into the revelation of Profound Reality's mercy, forgiveness, and a fresh start in being human. It was this revelation that knocked Saul off his horse, his high-horse of being a moralistic teacher into a whole new life of this new man who took the new name "Paul."

Perhaps the clearest resurrection narrative in the Gospels is the 24th chapter of Luke. Here is my take on this remarkable text: In this story, Cleopas and an unnamed disciple, perhaps a woman, are leaving the scene of Jesus' crucifixion in a state of despair. According to the story, they have already heard tales about an empty tomb and Jesus being alive, but this has made no impression on them. Clearly, these two despairing disciples were not even interested in a resurrection that may or may not have happened to Jesus. Only when the resurrection was something that happened to them personally did "it" become an event worth remembering.

So here they are walking down the road in despair, "their faces drawn in misery," and some mysterious figure they do not recognize begins to walk with them. In an almost jocular and nonchalant fashion this mystery figure gets them talking about what is bugging them. They express their grief in these poignant words, "But we were hoping that he (Jesus) was the one who was to come and set Israel free." So then this mysterious figure, whom we, the readers, are told is Jesus himself, does a theological interpretation for them on the subject of suffering. The main point of this sermon was the claim that it was befitting for the Christ "the expected one" to suffer. It is almost like Jesus is asking these two travelers this question, "Have you ever heard of a true prophet who did not suffer rejection?"

After this lecture on suffering, Luke, or whoever was the author of this story, inserts these words in his tale: "They were by now approaching the village to which they were going." Surely, this sentence is alluding to a "Spirit" destination that Luke is about to describe. Let us contemplate these power-packed words:

> *He* [the mystery figure] *gave the impression that he meant to go on further, but they stopped him with the words, "Do stay with us. It is nearly evening and soon the day will be over." So he went indoors to stay with them. THEN IT HAPPENED! While he was sitting at table with them he took the loaf, gave thanks, broke it and passed it to them. Their eyes opened wide and they knew him! But he vanished from their sight. Then they said to each other, "Weren't our hearts glowing* [burning] *while he was with us on the road and when he made the scriptures so plain to us?" And they got to their feet without delay and turned back to Jerusalem.*

They had just walked SEVEN MILES away from Jerusalem, from the scene of the crucifixion. But after IT HAPPENED, they walked back, without delay, at night fall, SEVEN MILES to the very place where their entire lives had come unraveled. We are left to assume that these two disciples joined the community of those who spent the rest of their lives celebrating rather than despairing over the fact that a true Messiah gets rejected by the fallen world.

Martin Luther King, Jr. provides us a recent example that can give us some understanding of what it means to reconcile humans to the Almighty Reality, to the God revered in both Old and New Testaments. We may have had difficulty sorting out what it means for Jesus to have died for our sins. But clearly Martin Luther King, Jr. died for our sins, for our racial estrangement. Whether we citizens of the United States were conscious or unconscious bigots who oppressed a portion of our citizenry, or whether we were among those who allowed ourselves to be outwardly and/or inwardly oppressed, King died for our sins. If we were willing to be changed, we were "born of his Spirit and washed in his blood." Martin King knew that he was risking his life. He knew he might be killed. He did not know when or how or whether, but he was aware that he might not enter the "promised land" of a better America. Nevertheless, he was willing to lay down his life that others might enter that land. The exact same dynamic applies to Jesus. We, humanity, [not Jews, not Romans, but humanity] killed the best of what humanity could be. The characteristic sin of that time was not African American racism, but a type of ingrown arrogance with regard to law and to a crushing moralism. Jesus challenged his times to the core and delivered many to new life. The part of his times that was not willing to accept his challenge, shed his blood. That blood was shed for us. The Almighty Reality was in Christ reconciling fallen humanity to the Almighty Reality. The Almighty was in Martin King reconciling fallen humanity to the Almighty. Notice again that this redemption was for the world—for each human and each human society, not just for Christians.

In the understandings of our century it is possible to see that the Almighty was also in the Moslem, Malcolm X, reconciling fallen humanity to the Almighty. The Almighty was in the Hindu, Gandhi, reconciling fallen humanity to the Almighty. We need to add to this list of men, some women like Harriet Tubman, Susan B. Anthony, and many others who flung their caring lives into the estrangement of their times and their sector of humanity. The Almighty Reality can be in any one of us reconciling fallen humanity to Almighty Reality. We are exploring here a universal dynamic of history, not a mere Christian dogma.

> Blessed Assurance Martin is mine, Jesus is mine!
> Oh what a foretaste of glory divine!
> Heir of salvation, purchase of God,
> Born of his Spirit, washed in his blood.

> This is my story, this is my song,
> Praising my Martin, my Jesus, my Harriet, my Susan,
> my whoever,
> all the day long.
> This is my story, this is my song,
> Praising my Healers all the day long.

I will conclude my survey of New Testament story telling with my introduction to my commentary on the Gospel of Mark. This commentary includes the complete text of Mark, my commentary upon it, and some discussion questions. It is available as a free download from the Realistic Living website:

https://realisticliving.org/blog/mark-commentary/

SESSION FIVE

Mark and the Molding of Christianity
An introduction to a Commentary on the Gospel of Mark

Living in Aramaic-speaking Galilee twenty-one centuries ago, Jesus and his first companions constituted the event of revelation that birthed the Christian faith. But without Paul's interpretation of the meaning of cross and resurrection for the Greek-speaking Hellenistic Jewish culture, we might never have heard of Christian faith. Mark, whoever he was, lived during the lifetime of Paul and was deeply influenced by Paul. In about 70 CE, Mark's Gospel was a major turning point in the development of the Christian religion. Mark invented the literary form we know as "the Gospel." This remarkable literary form was then copied and elaborated by the authors Matthew and Luke, and then revolutionized by John. These four writings, not Paul's letters, are the opening books of the New Testament that Christians count as their Bible (along with the Old Testament). "Gospel" (Good News) has become a name for the whole Christian revelation.

We might say that Mark was the theologian who gave us the Christianity that has survived in history. The Markian shift in Christian imagination was important enough that we might even claim that Mark, rather than Paul, Peter, or Jesus, was the founder of Christianity. However that may be, Mark's gospel is a very important piece of writing. And this writing is more profound and wondrous than is commonly appreciated.

Of first importance for understanding my viewpoint in the following commentary is this: I see the figure of "Jesus" in Mark's narrative as a fictitious character—based, I firmly believe, on a real historical figure. But I do not want to confuse Mark's "Jesus" with what we can know

213

through our best recent scientific research about the historical Jesus of Nazareth. For our best understanding of Mark, we need to view Mark's "Jesus" with the same fun and sensibility we have toward Harry Potter when we read J. K. Rowling's novels about that also unusual character.

In other words, Mark is the theologian that we are reading in the Gospel of Mark, not Jesus or Paul, and not Luke or Matthew or John. Mark is himself an unusually clever writer and a profound theologian. This truth is fundamental for understanding the following commentary.

> *What do you think about Mark being the creator of Christianity?*

> *How is it important to you that the historical Jesus of modern scholarship differs significantly from the Jesus of Mark's narrative?*

What is Theology?

Not all religions have a theology, but Judaism, Christianity, and Islam do. Buddhism has Dharma sutras and many Dharma talks that are still being given today. These thoughtful efforts of the Buddhist religion are something like a theology. It is fair to say that all religions have a "theoretics"—something that its members do to reflect upon the core topics that characterize that religion's ongoing community of thoughtfulness about their life together, their message, their mission, as well as their religious practices and ethical guidelines.

Christian theologizing begins its thoughtfulness with reflections upon a specific event (a specific complex of happenings in history). The happenings that constitute this "event" are understood to reveal the profound essence of every event in human history. That event has been given the name "Jesus Christ." An ordinary first century man named "Jesus," understood to be the "Messiah," was viewed as a revelation about living in an ultimate devotion to the Ultimate Reality that we encounter in every event of our personal lives, and in every event of our social history.

Judaism does something similar in its theologizing, but in this case the core revelatory event is "The Exodus from Egypt." Islam also treasures a revelatory event—in this case, "the Advent of Mohammad as a Messenger of the One Ultimate Creator of all things and events." Obviously, in each of these religious groupings, there is good theology and bad theology, depending on whether those theological reflections appropriately reflect what their revelatory event revealed about the essence of living a human life. Good theology also depends upon whether a particular bit of theological thoughtfulness has resonance with living people in their contemporary settings.

This commentary on the Gospel of Mark intends to be "theology" in the sense just defined. I prefer the word "theologizing," for I see Christian theology as an ongoing process of a community of people. My contribution to the ongoing process of Christian theologizing may be minor or large, but that is not entirely up to me. The community of those who are grounded in the Christ Jesus revelation will value or not value, preserve or not preserve, my contributions to the ongoing theologizing process of those who are captivated by the Christ Jesus revelation.

I see myself doing a radical form of Christian theologizing. It is "radical" because this thoughtfulness is my attempt to return to the "roots" of the Christian revelation from the perspective of a radically contemporary understanding of the nature and role of religion in human society.

"Religion," as I now understand that word, is not a set of stable doctrines and moralities allied with a once-and-for-all finished set of solitary and communal practices. The only stability that a religion has is its radical root. Religious doctrines and moralities, as well as religious practices are all in flux. Today, that flux is huge for every religion on Earth. The sort of Buddhism that is sweeping the North American continent is not stuck in the ruts of previous centuries. It is a fresh, creative accessing of Buddhism's ancient roots. In Christianity we are seeing something similar. I count this commentary part of that fresh effort to see the Christian revelation with new eyes and to hear this "good news" with new ears.

How in your life have you participated in Christian theologizing?

Whose theologizing has helped you most with your own theologizing?

The Death of a Metaphor

Some members of the Christian community speak of "the death of God" or even "the end of theology." In this commentary (and in all my theologizing), I take the view that "the death of God" does not refer to an end of all use of the word "God," I choose to understand "the death-of-God discussion" as pointing to the end of something temporal—namely, the obsolescence of an ancient metaphor of religious thinking held in the word "transcendence." For 2000 years Christian theologizing has used this familiar metaphorical narrative: a vivid story-time imagination about a transcendent realm in which God, angels, devils, gods, goddesses, and other story-time characters are living in an other-than-ordinary "realm" and "coming" from that "spiritual realm" to "act" within our ordinary human space and time. That is metaphorical talk. Being metaphorical, however, is not the problem. The problem for us today is the obsolete quality of that double-deck metaphor. Willy-nilly or intentionally we now reflect upon our lives in one universe, not two.

I am using an alternative metaphorical system of religious reflection in my mode of Biblical interpretation. I view our ordinary lives, as well as our profound lives, as participants in "One" realm of being. This "One Reality" has a depth that is invisible to both human eye and mind. I am using the capitalization of "Reality" to mean something different than our mind's "sense of reality." Reality is a "Land of Mystery" that the human mind cannot fathom. This profound depth of Reality shines through the passing realities of time that are visible to eye and mind. This Invisible Eternity can be said to "shine-through" temporal events. An ordinary bush can indeed burn with Eternity. An ordinary human being can indeed glow with the Presence of Eternity. But this Eternity is not another space that is separate from our ordinary space/time of living. Furthermore, this fresh view of Eternity does not imply a contempt for the temporal realm. Rather, it implies a fulfillment for each and every ordinary temporal event of our lives. Each temporal event has an Eternal depth or glow or burn. Eyes and ears alone cannot grasp our profound humanness and its Eternal connection. Only our enigmatic consciousness can "see" the Eternal, and this "seeing" is an internal experience that is "seen" in absolute solitude—a solitude that is happening as part of communities of people.

In this fresh context the words "ordinary" and "extraordinary" are viewed as mere categories of human perception. We live in One, and only One, realm of Reality with many temporally viewed aspects. Among these many aspects, we can speak of this basic polarity: the impermanent and the permanent—the temporal and the Eternal. This polarity is not in Reality itself, but in our human consciousness of Reality. Temporal and Eternal are both aspects of our one experience of one invisible One-ness that our minds cannot comprehend.

And this One-ness is not seen by eye or mind. We do not "see" One-ness directly. One-ness is a devotional category that means that we are devoted to serve all aspects of our Real experience, rather than viewing the Real as part friendly and part enemy. From this One-ness point of view, the only enemy is our own and other humans' estrangement from the One Reality, within which we and others dwell.

This One-ness viewpoint within Christian faith is not a denial of the diversity of our experiences of the Eternal or of the temporal nature of every "thing" in our lives—sun, moon, galaxy, husband, wife, chidden, everything. Differentiation and multiplicity obviously characterize our temporal lives. Multiplicity also characterizes much of our God-talk. In the God-talk of the Bible, there are many angels or servants of the One that express and carry out the actions of the One. But this One-ness is maintained in spite of the many-ness that is understood to be aspects of the Eternal, sourced from this One-ness. In the opening verses of the Bible, the One God says to some angels, "Let there be light!" and this was done by the One's many servant forces. Such poetry was intended to preserve the One-ness of Reality, not to fragment the One-ness of Reality that is fundamentally worshiped in the life of Christian faith.

How has it been hard or liberating for you to give up the old double-deck metaphor?

What has been your struggle with an overall devotion to One Ultimate Reality?

SESSION SIX

Interpreting Scripture Today

Today, Christian theologians, who want to go to the roots of the first century Christian "revelation," face the reality that people in the first century used the now obsolete two-tier, story-telling metaphor. That old manner of talking about ultimate matters had been the way of talking about ultimate matters for as long as anyone could remember.

In spite of the fact that their way of talking is no longer adequate for us today, we cannot claim to be Christians if we fail to interpret our scriptures. Therefore, to do scriptural interpretation adequately, we must translate for our era of culture what those early writers meant in their own lives when they used that old form of metaphorical talk that is now basically meaningless to us. Throughout this commentary, I will be illustrating what such metaphorical translation looks like.

Christian theologians today also face a second challenge. Within our current culture we tend to overlook metaphorical meanings altogether. We tend to view all statements literally. We learned to be literal from the current prominence of the scientific mode of truth. In the scientific style of thinking, words mean something only if words point to something in the realm of facts, observable by the human senses. Influenced by this overemphasis on facts, both religious agnostics and religious literalists fail to see the poetic or contemplative type of truth that is contained in the wild stories of the Bible. The agnostics are right to see that many stories of the Bible are preposterous when viewed literally. And religious literalists, who think they are defending Biblical truth with their literalism, are actually ignoring the profound truth that is hidden in these wildly creative stories.

For example, Mark tells a story about a 12-year-old Israelite girl being lifted from the dead, and his hearers could understand without qualms that this was a story about the 12 tribes of Israel being called back to life from a sleep-like-death. Listeners to such writing caught on to these metaphorical meanings without any need for help from a word like "metaphorical." Why? Their minds were not yet characterized by an overemphasis on literal truth.

Fictitious stories still mean a great deal to most of us today. Thousands of youth and adults have enjoyed deeply the stories of Harry Potter. We know that these are fiction, that Harry's magical ways are not to be taken literally. Yet we identify with him and his close friends in being magical persons who do not fit into the general society and who need to keep their true nature secret from most people. In other words, we can still see truth in fictitious stories, if we let ourselves do so. So as we read the Gospel of Mark, we need to keep in the forefront of our thinking that Mark is composing his "good news" in a hot-fiction mode of truth. We need to interpret Mark's preposterous story telling in a contemplative manner. In our dialogue with Mark, we are challenged to notice how we have had or can have these same life experiences in our own lives today.

How has literal biblical interpretation been a factor in your life?

What biblical poetry still puzzles you today?

Cross and Resurrection

It is fair to say that the symbols of cross and resurrection are as central to an understanding of the Christian revelation as meditation and enlightenment are to an understanding of Buddhism. Yet both cross and resurrection seem cryptic, even weird, to many people today.

Members of our current scientific culture may be excused somewhat for having a weak understanding of resurrection. Most of us know, if we are honest, that belief in a literal return to life of a three-day-old corpse is superstition. Yet this meaning of resurrection has been paraded as Christian by many interpreters of the resurrection symbol. Mark did not see resurrection in this light. Or perhaps we might better say, "Mark did not see resurrection in this darkness," for a literal return from the dead means nothing deeply religious to Mark or to you or me. If such an event were to happen today, it would be open to hundreds of speculative explanations, none of which would be profoundly or convincingly religious.

Mark's understanding of the cross is equally opaque in our culture. Some modern authors even accuse Christianity of having a morbid preoccupation with death, suffering, and tragedy. The crucifix, or even a bare cross, is viewed by some as silly and grim—like hanging a guillotine on your wall or around your neck. But for Mark the horror of the cross is seen as priceless food for the soul. How can that be? Surely, we have some thoughtful exploration to do, if we are to grasp the Gospel (the good news) that Mark claims to be announcing.

I know of no better way to introduce the symbols of cross and resurrection to a contemporary explorer of Christianity than with a commentary of Mark's Gospel. I will show in this commentary that Mark understands the resurrection as intimately- connected with the cross and that both are about possible experiences that every human being can have. As characters in Mark's Gospel, the disciples do not experience the fullness of resurrection until the very last chapter of Mark's narrative. Until then, resurrection for them is a secret. At the same time Jesus experiences resurrection in the first 13 verses of Mark's commentary. For the rest of this narrative, Jesus is what a resurrected person looks like walking, talking, eating, sleeping, praying, healing others, and challenging the status quo. The character Jesus in Mark's Gospel is an exemplar of living the resurrected life unto death

Meanwhile the disciples are what it looks like to be on a journey toward resurrection. They are dramatized as dumb dumbs on both cross and resurrection. So we can view Mark's narrative as about two journeys that are both aspects of our own life journey: (1) the journey of spirit awakening that is taking place in the lives of the disciples and (2) the journey of the spirit-awake human—what that looks like in action —that is, how Jesus' presence, words, and actions are dramatizing the qualities of the resurrected human and how such a presence among us is healing to others. The full meaning of the resurrection will remain Mark's secret until chapter 16, but cross and resurrection are primary symbols in Mark's narrative beginning in chapter one.

Again, both these journeys can go on in the lives of all of us: (1) we, like the disciples, can journey toward full enlightenment (death-and-resurrection living), and (2) we, like Jesus, can resolve to live our resurrection life (spirit enlightenment or profound humanness) in the real world, in the historical challenges of our time and place. As resurrected women and men, we, like Jesus can expend our new life of profound humanness for the healing and well-being of others. We are invited to identify with both Jesus and the disciples in Mark's narrative.

In the first 13 verses of chapter one, Mark's character "Jesus" has his own death and resurrection experience—in the same sense that you or I might have our own death and resurrection experience—in the living now of our own conscious lives. It is important to notice that Mark retains the complete humanness of Jesus by having him in these early verses undergo John's baptism of spirit washing and Jesus' own calling to spirit mission, a calling that any of us might also experience.

After those first 13 verses, Mark's Jesus is on a different journey than the disciples. The disciples are on a spirit journey toward resurrection.

Jesus depicts the journey of the resurrected human in action. He is what a human being looks like who has been resurrected to his or her profound humanness, after having died to his or her temporal relations as his or her primal devotion. I repeat, Mark's Jesus-story is about the journey unto death of a human being after entry into the resurrected life.

In Luke's second book, *The Acts of the Apostles*, we see more about what this second journey of living the life of resurrected humans looks like as the story of real-world historical persons other than Jesus. Peter, Paul and other men and women are presented by Luke as further "resurrection" exemplars. Luke wants us to get it that we who live "in Christ" are living the resurrection life. Indeed, we are to be the resurrection of Jesus. We are called to be the body that rose on Easter morning.

It is probably easier for most of us to identify with the disciples who are moving toward resurrection step-by-step through the course of Mark's story. We can also identify with the crowds who are intrigued, but puzzled, by Jesus' parables. We can even identify with those persons who reject Jesus.

Mark's Jesus uses parables to trick the sleeping into noticing their sleepiness and into seeking more truth. Then to his more committed disciples, Mark's Jesus explains his parables further, expecting them to catch on to their own profound humanness sooner than the crowds.

Mark is assuming that the readers of his Gospel will be carried along, like the disciples, toward the total unraveling of their egoism to an embodiment of the resurrected life that was walking and talking among them in the body of Jesus and later in the body of the church, that came to be referred to as "the body of Christ"—that is, the body of the resurrected one. So in Mark's narrative, we are entitled to identify with Jesus ministering to his blind followers as well as with we identifying with the blind followers to whom Jesus is ministering.

As we read Mark's gospel, let us keep in mind the originality and imagination of this remarkable person we are calling "Mark." We are dialoguing with Mark, not with Jesus. Jesus is a character in Mark's story. We are in a conversation with Mark in the same way that reading a Harry Potter novel is a conversation with J. K. Rowling, rather than Harry Potter. Of course we can have a conversation with Harry Potter as one of Rowling's characters. Similarly, we can have a conversation with Jesus as one of Mark's characters.

In the following commentary, here is what I am going to do. I am going to quote in order the entire Markian text. After each section of Mark's narrative, I will do a commentary on the quoted verses and follow that with a few discussion questions. I am assuming the best of New Testament historical scholarship, but I will be doing what I call "21st century theologizing for the ordinary reader."

So what are you looking forward to in this study?

And what puzzles you most about this enigmatic document called "The Gospel of Mark"?

The Scripture quotations from Mark's Gospel are taken from J. B. Phillips translation. I have chosen this version because of its ordinary and personally effective language. While there may be better translations of the literal Greek, it is also true that Mark used a street Greek. Mark spoke in ordinary speech to ordinary people. Most of the first hearers of Mark's text heard it read aloud. J. B. Phillips captures, I believe, this sense of ordinary story telling. Again, this entire commentary is available as a free download from the Realistic Living website: https://realisticliving.org/blog/mark-commentary/ I recommend this volume for further study of New Testament stories.

D. OUR ONGOING STORY TELLING

D EAR READER. IF YOU FOUND for yourself in these two courses of introduction to the Old and New Testament Scriptures of Christian theologizing Good News, you can teach these two courses. Each of us, including me, can understand these introductions more deeply by teaching them. And perhaps even more important, we allow more people to see for themselves that we do not have to read the Bible through the eyes of people conserving an obsolete view of this important religion.

Teaching the Bible is a basic witnessing love for others, and most of us are called to be teachers in that regard. Just find 5 to 12 people to meet with you in your living room or somewhere else for the required number of one hour sessions. Start with the Old Testament introductory course. The New Testament introductory course is built on the foundation of the Old. The ongoing theologizing of the Christian Good News is build upon the foundation of the whole Christian Bible. We need to start with a radical renewal or an introduction of new people to this religious practice and its healing benefits.

Here is a simple way to proceed. Have your small class read the reading for each session before the class session. And then during the class have portions of the text read aloud and then ask a relevant question of your class. Start with an easy to answer question like: *What phrase or sentence in the text did you find noteworthy?* Follow up with a more personal question like: *How does any of this section ask you to consider this topic differently.* Continue with: *What about this is personally challenging?* And *What more needs to said?*

Simply prompt an intimate conversation. Don't argue. Don't demand your preferred responses. Let Profound Reality do the deep teaching. You are just a means of grace, not the Grace of the Eternal Good News itself. Grace is given by the Eternal to those who are ready for it. Do not presume to know who those persons are or when they are going to be ready to receive this Grace.

You can insist, however, on having a group conversation. Ask each person to speak. Encourage people to have their real responses and feelings. Everything anyone says may be helpful. Share your own feeling and findings, but do not over talk the group. You can do this. And with these elemental teachings, we are overcoming a huge problem. Too many people are unfamiliar with the real Christian Scriptures. Too many people are dismissing these powerful resources, because so much poor interpretation has come their way.

However new or challenging this Good News may seem to members of your class, honesty is what you want from the class. Their doubts and questions are sacred. If this does not seem like Good News to them, you can maintain that their discovering their doubts and questions is Good News for now. It may take several sessions before some members of each class can see most of these passages as Good News. And classes are needed. It takes time and companionship to hear this Good News. Oral talks help, but studying together helps more. And the study is not over in one course. Such study goes on throughout the life of a Christian practice.

Also, you will be teaching the skill of theologizing for ourselves a well as assisting in the proclamation of the Good News that is contained in these Scriptures. You are also maintaining that the future of a healthy

Christian communal life depends upon our recovery of the Scriptures. Without a living Bible there is no renewal of the Christian faith. This is just as true as the statement that without some living experiences of meditative practice, there is no renewal of Buddhism. Like doing meditation, hearing the stories of the Bible is a religious practice that makes enlightenment more likely.

Nevertheless, it takes time and persistence to awaken both current Christian practitioners and current non-Christians to the wonders of the Bible. This is so because the Bible has been mistakenly interpreted for a number of generations. So we in our culture are in the situation of having both the clinging to corrupt interpretations of the Bible and a big horror of the Bible because of these corruptions. It is also true that many people in our current culture have almost no vivid memories of these Biblical stories. To many the Bible has become a foreign language they have never learned.

Christian scriptures are very old, and require scholarship of the historical life situations of these texts. Also required is the relation of our life to the lives of the biblical authors, and the relation of their lives to our lives. This is a matter of human existence, not just words, words, words. We may get help from a dictionary, but mostly we get our help from our own lives. The Word of God is heard directly from the Profound Reality we are honoring with the word "God."

Also, Christian theologizing did not end with the New Testament. Augustine's voluminous 5th century writings is the climax of almost four more centuries of intense Christian thoughtfulness. Augustine's basic overview of theologizing guidelines lasted in latin-speaking Europe for another eight hundred years. In the 13th century, Thomas Aquinas 's voluminous writings produced a shift from the Augustinian era of Plotinus enriched theologizing to a theologizing that used the Aristotelian import of philosophical ideas found alive in the Muslim world. In the 15th century Luther's voluminous writings gave a new energy to this history.

In the 20th Century a host of great theologians picked up on the the 19th century Christian theologizing of Søren Kierkegaard who was also a philosopher of importance in helping to initiate an existentialist period in philosophy. The 20th Century theologians in the Kierkegaardian wake include Karl Barth, Paul Tillich, Rudolf Bultmann, Dietrich Bonhoeffer, H.Richard Niebuhr and his brother Reinhold. A further participation in existential theologizing has been done by Roman Catholics luminaries such as Karl Rhaner, Thomas Merton, Thomas Berry, and others. We also have many women joining this list of great theologians, Simone Weil, Suzanne DeDietrich, Dorothee Soelle, Mary Daly, Sabine Dramm, and others.

My mentor Joe Mathews was a wonderful teacher of many of these resources. I have sought to extend his 20th century wake-up calls into the 21st Century confrontations in philosophy, ecology, feminism, an interfaith religious world, and for political, economic and cultural ethical challenges for as troubling a 21st century world as we could ever have even imagined in earlier times.

In the 21st Century, one of our most popular detours into theological unrealism has been viewing theological thoughtfulness as simply a philosophy of life among other philosophies of life, each of them an approximate truth at best and a misleading rationalism at worst. I am especially concerned for us not to be led astray by "To each his own truth—as if there were no truth upon which a universal sort of confidence can be grounded. There is indeed no "heaven of reason" that judges all our favored reasonings. I am going to continue arguing the case that a revelation-less direction for Christian theologizing is a detour from the roadway of good theologizing of the Christian revelation of a Ground of Being or Profound Reality that does indeed judge all our approximate knowing and all our rational speculations.

Furthermore, Christian theologizing has become a religious practice done not only by the expert scholars for whole societies, but also by every member of small circles of Christian ex-clergy and ex-laity meeting together on a weekly basis as co-pastors to one another and as a co-pastorate to some local community of this planet. It is mostly for these small circles that I write. I wish to help us steer out of the ditches of "my own philosophies of life" into the realistic roadways of revealed Truth concerning Profound Reality's love for each of us—benefiting to each of us in support of our own authentic living and thinking about living. Our ongoing Christian theological story telling needs to continue a revealed truthfulness in communities of being pastor to each other in small circles that never again seek to become large denominations, or hold some master dogma or master morality or even a master theology for a whole society or a top-down organization of any sort.

Christian theologizing of high quality can and must take place among common men and women, as well as the scholars, if we are ever to have a next Christianity that replaces the corruptions of the current forms of Christian religion.

A POSTSCRIPT ON APPROXIMATE KNOWING

Theologizing and Organizing

Part One of this book is about some general thoughtfulness on philosophizing, especially on the topic of truth and on our human approaches to truth. I am not a professional philosophizer unless a few dollars of book royalty count, but I have studied philosophy intently. I am especially interested in a philosophy of the disciplines of learning and how they relate to one another and to the thoughtfulness of theologizing.

Part Two of this book is about a philosophy of religion, especially how we can see effective religion as an essential social process in every society—a lack of which or a perversion of which is a disaster for that society. This has entailed looking into deep history to see an antiquity of religious metaphors that are primal in their nature. Each of these primal metaphors were a type of revelation or enlightenment about some aspect of our human awareness of Profound Reality. A human society does not flourish without such anchors in Profound Reality.

Part Three of this book is about the radical renewal of a particular religion—Christianity, my own practice, my own radical form of that practice. I am using the word "radical" to mean "returning to the roots." I have argued that we must return to our Old and New Testament revelation stories, hear them anew, and come forward from there in our theological thoughtfulness, religious practices, and ethical guidelines.

When we have built a constituency of religious study at this level of relevance within our local place, we will be ready to invite a group of companions to explore a new style of Christian practice that takes seriously small group honesty and a depth probing of human life within a foundation of thoughtful spirit community that breaths the Holy Spirit that has from time two time made Christian faith a core contribution to life in general. For suggestions along those lines see Part Three of my earlier book *The Thinking Christian.*

OTHER BOOKS BY GENE MARSHALL

In 2020, I published with Wipf and Stock a 398-page pull together of my earlier teachings and writings: *The Thinking Christian: Twenty-three Pathways of Awareness.* Part One of *The Thinking Christian* introduces the overall religious revolution taking place planet wide. Part Two introduces Christian theologizing for this interfaith context of world cultures; I am using the word "theologizing" to indicate that Christian thoughtfulness is an ongoing group practice rather than a static theology of this or that theologian. Part Three is about visions for new wineskins of ethical and communal life for the wine of the 20th Century Theological Revolution and its uprooted millions. This new communal life enables both a deeper nurture of the group and a better ethical process for service to the world in which we dwell.

I also want to alert you to four other books published with iUniverse:

(1) 2003 *The Call of the Awe: Rediscovering Christian Profundity in an Inter-religious Era.* This book views Christianity in contrast with the long-standing religions of our deep past.

(2) 2009 *Jacob's Dream: A Christian Inquiry into Spirit Realization.* This book uses the enneagram personality types as a clue to a better understanding the human falling into unreality and then being restored to our essential freedom.

(3) 2011 *The Road from Empire to Eco-Democracy is* a secular ethics book that is still relevant in the time of Trump. Over a four year period, I coauthored this book with Ben Ball, Marsha Buck, Ken Kreutziger, and Alan Richard This book was also jointly published as an Open Book Editions with Berrett-Koehler Publishers.

(4) 2015 *The Enigma of Consciousness: A Philosophy of Profound Humanness and Religion,* a secular book on religion and ethics for humans seeking profoundness.

In 2014 with Resurgence Publishing, I ventured to write a book on Christian church history: *The Love of History and the Future of Christianity: Toward a Manifesto for a Next Christianity.* Though I am not a historical scholar, this narrative is a good study book for an introduction to the importance of history in Christian theologizing.

In 2023 I published with the Rosedog imprint of Dorrance Publishing *So Be Free: Pastoral Discourses on Freedom.* Does freedom exist or are we totally determined?

In 2019 I published as a free download on the Realistic Living website a book on New Testament interpretation: *The Creator of Christianity: A Commentary on the Gospel of Mark.* Every verse of Mark is quoted, commentary made, and discussion questions asked. To download this study book go to: *https://realisticliving.org/blog/mark-commentary/*

In 2018, I published with a Canadian company WoodLake *Radical Gifts: Living the Full Christian Life in Troubled Times.* WoodLake is now closed down, and the remaining copies of this excellent study book are owned by me. For further information go to: *https://realisticliving.org/radical-gifts/*

Printed in the United States
by Baker & Taylor Publisher Services